Cambridge Elements

Elements in Histories of Emotions and the Senses
edited by
Rob Boddice
Tampere University
Piroska Nagy
Université du Québec à Montréal (UQAM)
Mark Smith
University of South Carolina

EMBODIED EPISTEMOLOGY AS RIGOROUS HISTORICAL METHOD

Lauren Mancia
*Brooklyn College and The Graduate Center
City University of New York (CUNY)*

Shaftesbury Road, Cambridge CB2 8EA, United Kingdom

One Liberty Plaza, 20th Floor, New York, NY 10006, USA

477 Williamstown Road, Port Melbourne, VIC 3207, Australia

314–321, 3rd Floor, Plot 3, Splendor Forum, Jasola District Centre,
New Delhi – 110025, India

103 Penang Road, #05–06/07, Visioncrest Commercial, Singapore 238467

Cambridge University Press is part of Cambridge University Press & Assessment, a department of the University of Cambridge.

We share the University's mission to contribute to society through the pursuit of education, learning and research at the highest international levels of excellence.

www.cambridge.org
Information on this title: www.cambridge.org/9781009590358

DOI: 10.1017/9781009590334

© Lauren Mancia 2025

This publication is in copyright. Subject to statutory exception and to the provisions of relevant collective licensing agreements, no reproduction of any part may take place without the written permission of Cambridge University Press & Assessment.

When citing this work, please include a reference to the DOI 10.1017/9781009590334

First published 2025

A catalogue record for this publication is available from the British Library

ISBN 978-1-009-59035-8 Hardback
ISBN 978-1-009-59032-7 Paperback
ISSN 2632-1068 (online)
ISSN 2632-105X (print)

Additional resources for this publication at www.cambridge.org/HOES_Mancia

Cambridge University Press & Assessment has no responsibility for the persistence or accuracy of URLs for external or third-party internet websites referred to in this publication and does not guarantee that any content on such websites is, or will remain, accurate or appropriate.

For EU product safety concerns, contact us at Calle de José Abascal, 56, 1°, 28003 Madrid, Spain, or email eugpsr@cambridge.org

Embodied Epistemology as Rigorous Historical Method

Elements in Histories of Emotions and the Senses

DOI: 10.1017/9781009590334
First published online: May 2025

Lauren Mancia
*Brooklyn College and The Graduate Center
City University of New York (CUNY)*

Author for correspondence: Lauren Mancia, laurenmancia@brooklyn.cuny.edu

Abstract: This Element proposes that, in addition to using traditional historical methodologies, historians need to find extra-textual, embodied ways of understanding the past in order to more fully comprehend it. Written by a medieval historian, the Element explains why historians assume they cannot use reperformance in historical inquiry and why they, in fact, should. The Element employs tools from the discipline of performance studies, which has long grappled with the differences between the archive and the repertoire, between the records of historical performances and the embodied movements, memories, and emotions of the performance itself, which are often deemed unknowable by scholars. It shows how an embodied epistemology is particularly suited to studying certain premodern historical topics, using the example of medieval monasticism. Finally, using the case of performance-lectures given at The Met Cloisters, it shows how using performance as a tool for historical investigation might work.

Keywords: embodiment, historiography, performance studies, medieval studies, religious studies

© Lauren Mancia 2025

ISBNs: 9781009590358 (HB), 9781009590327 (PB), 9781009590334 (OC)
ISSNs: 2632-1068 (online), 2632-105X (print)

Contents

1 Why This Method: A Personal Introduction — 1

2 Why Do We Assume We *Cannot* Use Performance in Historical Inquiry? — 5

3 Why We *Should* Use Performance in Historical Inquiry — 13

4 How Embodied Epistemology Is Particularly Suited to Studying Certain Historical Topics: The Example of Medieval Monasticism — 21

5 How Can We Use Performance? The Case of Performance-Lectures in The Met Cloisters — 28

References — 53

Embodied Epistemology as Historical Method

> The world of knowledge takes a crazy turn /when teachers themselves are taught to learn.
> Bertolt Brecht (Preston, 2016, p. 149)

> Do it, do it, and then you find out what the heck it is. A posteriori, a priori, whatever.
> Carmelita Tropicana (Troyano, 2000, p. 177)

1 Why This Method: A Personal Introduction

Ever since I got into medieval history as an undergraduate, I have been trying to answer the question: How did it *feel* to *do* medieval devotional practices? There are simple answers to this question, and there are complicated ones. For instance, it is uncontroversial to outline the total experiential *setting* a medieval person would have encountered in a church: We can easily enumerate and describe a historical space and its liturgical furnishings, music, lighting, and readings, and art historians, liturgists, and musicologists have been particularly good at this kind of interdisciplinary work (Nelson, 2007; Schleif, 2009; Fassler, 2010; Mariani, 2017; Jung, 2020; Peers, 2020; Pentcheva, 2020; Caldwell, 2022). Theater scholars likewise animate play texts by experimenting with them in performance, "standing them up" and not merely reading them silently (Vitz, 2014; Dutton, 2019; Sergi, 2020; Blanc, 2024). Scholars also regularly feel able to answer this question with citations from texts, noting how "eyewitnesses *say* that it felt like *x*," and appending the necessary disclaimer about texts being discursive performances for the audiences that consumed them, more than accurate descriptions of interior "reality."

Interior "reality" – this is where answers to my question start getting complicated. If texts are discursive rather than real expressions of inner life, the question of what was *really* historically experienced emotionally versus what people *said* they experienced is an eternal distinction that haunts historians. After all, scholars often comment, how much do we each even know about the inner reality we *ourselves* are experiencing anyway, let alone that of *historical* people! Aren't all of our feelings mediated by psychology, memory, and the discursive forces of our respective zeitgeists? Moreover, as a medievalist especially, I would add that it is incredibly difficult to strip away the forces of modernity from our understanding of the experiences of people 1,000 years ago. Every historian knows that "the question of experience can be approached nowadays only with an acknowledgment that it is no longer accessible to us" (Agamben, 2007, p. 15).

My desire to recover historical inner experience is made even more hopeless by the fact that what I want to investigate is the experience of a past person's *religion* particularly. I am a scholar who studies monastic devotional practices in the eleventh and twelfth centuries; I study coenobitic Benedictine monks who lived in communities, that is, the very anonymous, unindividuated monks that reformers like Bernard of Clairvaux, Francis of Assisi, and Martin Luther attacked for being too wealthy, too unthinking, and too duplicitous in their piety. *These* are the people whose inner religious experience I seek to better understand. Were I to be interested in the historical experiences of a different kind – someone whose gender, or servitude, or lordship I wanted to explore – there would likely be wider sympathy for my work in the secular academy. But in our day and age, religion *qua* religion (especially collective religion) is a hard pill for many academics to swallow; secular, left-leaning academics especially have grown so deeply uncomfortable with the notion that religion could be something other than a tool used by an institution seeking dominance and hegemony that they regularly ignore how it might also have been a genuine, authentic, emotional commitment by millions of historical people. So a conundrum remains: "religion is at once a false theory about the world and a way of experiencing it" (Mahmood, 2011, p. 14) – it is inevitably political *and* believed, both. In such a predicament, how do we attempt to get at the complex inner experience of medieval religious people?

In the centuries immediately following the European Middle Ages, scholars investigating medieval religion, art, music, devotional practices, theology, and spirituality were regularly themselves members of Catholic religious communities. In the last 100 years of historiography, much of their work has been glossed over as the work of biased historians writing auto-histories of their orders and their Church. Secular historians who are not themselves Catholic feel that they are better positioned to see the "truth" about medieval Christianity, so they by and large write through a cynical lens, talking about the Crusades as colonialism, the Church as power-hungry, and monasticism as Groupthink.[1] I am neither a nun nor a Christian, and as a historian, my *modus operandi* is to fully acknowledge, incorporate, and then ultimately go deeper than such cynical explanations in my work; and yet, I still *regularly* have to remind secular scholarly audiences at conferences and academic lectures of the potentially genuine religious motivations of my historical subjects. Audience members often ask me questions with cocked eyebrows ("Did that abbot *really* use the prayers he wrote, or did he just write them to lure his monastic brethren under his sway?"). Audiences also often suspect me of being devout myself, regularly

---

[1] Rachel Fulton Brown has described this: "our scholarship has privileged those who would look *at* devotion as something to be explained from the outside, rather than allowing ourselves to look *along* devotion to see what the devout might see ... If we want to understand the experience, we need some way of partaking in it, not just looking at it from the outside." (Fulton Brown, 2017, pp. xxix, xxx) While her critique of the academy here is valid, unlike me, Fulton Brown writes from her perspective as a "believing Christian," and so our solutions to this issue diverge (Fulton Brown, 2017, p. xviii).

asking me where I go to church (I don't) or how my work interacts with and supports my faith (it doesn't); they cannot conceive of a historian who has been trained by three separate secular institutions being interested in the inner experience of medieval monastic belief and devotional feeling, even though religion has been studied this way for some time by certain historians of religion (for instance, Jackson & Marotti, 2004).[2]

For the last ten years, I have used approaches recognized as "good" and "rigorous" by historians to study and compose arguments about my historical subjects (e.g., close reading, textual analysis, manuscript study, methods from the textually based history of emotions sub-field, etc.) (Mancia, 2019, 2023). I now think that something radical has to change about the way I perform and convey my scholarship: my rational arguments are not effective enough in convincing my audiences that there were, indeed, genuine emotional and spiritual experiences to be had in the practice of medieval monasticism. Moreover, I suspect that by making modern audiences *do* premodern behaviors, we can begin to disarm audiences' modern conceptions of the past, allowing us all to see premodern spirituality in a way that is less mediated by our modern gaze, and to feel a part of that historical inner experience that is not extractable from textual primary sources alone.

It dawned on me last year that my problem might be that up to now I have only *intellectually* described medieval devotion, engaging my audiences with precisely the wrong (critical) faculties to make a point about something that was, historically, *experiential*. This approach is, of course, the gold standard of professional history writing: it is a safe, empirical, "scientific," reason-led avenue of inquiry carved out initially by Hume in the eighteenth century and perpetuated by the nineteenth-century German *Wissenschaft* model, the pursuit of "objective" knowledge held fast to by contemporary historians of religion, especially those who hope to survive in the secular university by insisting that theirs is an impassive academic study (Pellegrini, 2009, p. 200; Gharavi, 2013, p. 210). But if I want my work to argue that medieval monks cultivated their own beliefs through active *doing* alongside rational *thinking*, that they weren't brainwashed but instead *practiced* their way into believing, shouldn't my method of argumentation be an argument of *doing* rather than *thinking*? Shouldn't it NOT be a presentation of a rational argument for passive consumption by the scholarly reader? Wouldn't it be more effective if I made my

---

[2] This line of questioning – assuming that because I study religion I must be religious – may be more about contemporary identity politics than anything medieval. Reginald Jackson has noted something similar about queer identities, stating that many assume he identifies as queer since he studies queer history (Jackson, 2021).

scholarly readers *do* what monks did in order to demonstrate *through experience* how monasticism worked?

In this Element, I will argue that impassive academic study is not enough to access historical experience – especially premodern religious experience. If we want to understand if and how coenobitic monks felt connected to what they were enacting, we need to change the ways we explore this history, going beyond textual evidence and turning to the "traces" of embodied dynamics of experience cultivated by medieval monastic ritual (Sponsler, 2017). We need to use an *embodied* epistemology alongside our cognitive one.

Monastic performance was relational and communal, involving and transporting everyone present toward inner meaning through embodied action. Monks themselves were what we would today call "performance researchers," using embodiment and performance to actively construct their visions, beliefs, and states of mind. They literally practiced what was preached so that they could understand it. The doing was a technique: "*Tu le crois si tu le fais, et si tu ne le fais pas, tu n'y crois pas*" (de Certeau, 1981, p. 367). Even if a monk harbored kernels of doubt, the shaping, molding, and crafting involved in an embodied religious life made a way of knowing that was totally different from that practiced in the modern American academy today. As historians, we neglect the "*body* of knowledge" (Dinshaw, 2012, p. 22) that was so essential to medieval monastic life because of our historiographical biases: because to reperform monastic actions would violate the purposely disembodied methods that our discipline has practiced for at least two hundred years.

Historians are hesitant to reperform and embody religious practices for some good reasons – we certainly do not want to misappropriate something that is not ours (Kirshenblatt-Gimblett, 1998; Madison, 2005). But we're also equally scared that by actively participating in embodied knowledge, we will be accused of trying to do something *unacademic* and will be laughed out of the professional academy. We make ourselves immune to the affects of doing so as not to bias our "objective" analyses (Schaefer, 2022). Even though scholars acknowledge medieval religion was "performative," we have a paltry understanding of what performance does – much less what it did 1,000 years ago for believers who witnessed and participated in it – because we never try it out for ourselves. If we want to understand if and how medieval people felt connected to what they were enacting, we need to change the ways historians explore this history, going beyond textual evidence and resuscitating the "traces" of embodied experience cultivated by medieval religious ritual and present in medieval sources (Taylor, 2003). We need to use *performance* to *do* history – and we need to see it as a rigorous historical method, a method for legitimate research, not just for teaching our students. More importantly, we need to acknowledge that we miss things as historians by *not* using performance to do history. We still need our age-old rigorous archival research methods to reveal medieval practices, to be sure; but, if we don't embody what we find in the archive, do we even fully understand what we're reading?

2 Why Do We Assume We *Cannot* Use Performance in Historical Inquiry?

2.1 Ranke and the Discipline of "Scientific" History

Since history's official formation as a discipline in the nineteenth century, historians in history departments have held firm to the notion that *responsible* history was *professional* history.[3] For too long in the Western world, history writing had been placed in the hands of amateurs who were too prone to romanticizing the past or using it to push biased agendas (Wood & Loud, 1991; Smith, 1998; Hen & Innes, 2000). History needed a scientific approach, and Leopold von Ranke's prescription – history *"wie es eigentlich gewesen,"* the past as it actually happened, without any judgment or elaboration – became the foundation of that method (Woolf, 2019, pp. 173–212). Ranke's more scientific approach caused historians to be deeply skeptical of "grand theory," elevating primary sources – written, archival sources (Smail, 2021, p. 8) – as the only evidence that mattered, as if these made "past events objectively available for discovery, description, and interpretation" (Kleinberg, 2020, pp. 157–165). Over the course of 200 years, historians have consistently promoted written source evidence as the premiere raw data, creating in the discipline of history a kind of "cult of objectivity" (Novick, 1988; Woolf, 2019, p. 217); despite the normal disciplinary ebbs, flows, and fads, the underlying current of history has remained "an empiricist enterprise … intrinsically linked to … an unquestioned allegiance to 'ontological realism'" (Biddick, 1998, pp. 1–3; Kleinberg, 2020, pp. 157–165; Fricke, 2022). As theorist Vanita Seth characterizes it, "since history's establishment as a discipline in the nineteenth century, the core, enabling presumption, upon which the discipline of history anchors its authority, is that there exists a past independent of human efforts to represent it" (Seth, 2024, pp. 128–129).

Why this clinging to documentary evidence? What was such attachment to "scientifically" knowable history saving Western historians from? Firstly, people in the Protestant Reformation, the Enlightenment, and the French

---

[3] When I say "historians," here, I am talking especially about scholars who have been trained in history departments. The methods and historiography I describe here has been less applicable for literary historians (in English departments) or art historians (in art history departments); it may even be less applicable for historians doing applied history (at military academies or fashion institutes, for instance, where military or fashion history is learned for a practical purpose).

Revolution attacked the medieval Church historians who had dominated early Western history writing as "irrational practitioners" aiming to hoodwink the masses and impose elite Church power. Newly disciplined ("Enlightened") historians chose to fight against this religious past, so they engaged in the opposite path, "rational" scientific history, far from the magic-filled, biased, and romanticized chronicles of medieval Church historians (McCutcheon, 2003; Woolf, 2019). Historical practice in Western Europe became a quest in unearthing the "authenticity" of the past – what had *really* happened, not what the Church *said* happened (Trilling, 1973; Umbrach, 2018). A professional historian was one who worked hard against any hint at a "slide to subjectivism" (Taylor, 2018, p. 55), one who aimed to "investigate the unseen real by inspecting fakes" (McCrary, 2022, pp. 43–51). Secondly, document-based analysis was a refuge from the threat of the inexplicable that so haunted the premodern landscape in the estimation of Enlightenment thinkers. It provided sure answers about why things happened in the past and what their causes and results were, after a period when premoderns had chalked so much up to supernatural and metaphysical forces (Bordo, 1987; Sternhell, 2023). Rationality would make all known, clear, and understood, and would triumph over the base animality of the body that supposedly defined premodern people (Huizinga, 1954, p. 9; Rosenwein, 2006, pp. 1–12). Intellectual, textual, *disembodied* thinking was pronounced the route to the truth.

Even historians who proposed practices to counter or nuance Ranke's historical method still claimed history to ultimately be objectively knowable in one way or another – scientific history maintained "an active life in our disciplinary unconscious" (Moxey, 2013, p. 23). Marxist historians in the early twentieth century made politics into a science that based every political action on a "strictly objective assessment of the social conditions in which it has to operate" (Polanyi, 1974, pp. 236–237, 239). Social and cultural historians, like Natalie Zemon Davis, looked for evidence, rules, habits, and historical coherence in the literary artifacts of the past, even as they pleaded that historians not "peel away" the "fictive elements in our documents so we could get at the 'real facts'" (Davis, 1990, pp. 3, 4). After the Linguistic Turn and the advent of Foucault, Derrida, and Spivak, historians began to cast texts as discursive constructions reflecting social logics rather than a series of true facts. But this focus on discourse was yet another peeling away, a conceptualization that comforted historians in knowing that they had revealed a truth about power and control in the past (Smith, 1999). Each historical subject became a "discursive conglomerate of socio-cultural practices" (Bentacourt, 2016, p. 4) deemed as knowable, their actions regularly cast as indicative of what was *really* going on in their sociocultural contexts (Burke, 2005). So, even as historians corrected Ranke's nineteenth-century positivist course, history was still "supposed to hold the past in place, in an order leading to the present in coherent narrative form" (Buck-Morrs, 2021, p. 1) – a narrative form no longer about "facts," perhaps, but instead about lived discourses. Moreover, the embrace of Marxist, Foucauldian, or other grand ideas by professional historians made textual sources – linguistic sources, whose semiotics were laid bare – become even more emphatically asserted as the only sources that historians could fully examine to uncover the discourses of the past (Spiegel, 1997, p. 22; Schneider, 2014, pp. 13, 21). In other words, even as historians recognize that texts are not transparent, we still cling to them and implicitly trust them *more* than nontextual materials.

The biggest consequence of these historiographical developments is that a majority of twentieth-century historians became more reluctant to attempt to uncover inner historical experiences. It should be noted that historians regularly use the phrase "historical experience" in tremendously casual ways, employing it to hypothesize how a historical person might have encountered a temple (they "experienced" the space), or developed political strategies after a revolt (they "learned from experience"), or neurologically processed an emotion (they "experienced longing" for their child in exile), for example. But what historians became increasingly reluctant to do was to describe "the intersection between public language and private subjectivity, between expressible commonalities and the ineffability of the individual interior" (Jay, 2005, p. 41). Historians could analyze the ritualized prescriptions of clerics and kings and could unpack the discourses alive in normative texts. What they could not do was attempt to describe what Jay calls "ineffable," how it *felt* to be subjected to those texts in the past, to live those texts in history.

Throughout the twentieth century, certain subdisciplines in the fields of archeology (called "experimental archeology"), anthropology (called "anthropology of experience"), and religion (called "lived religion") developed techniques to get closer and closer to a responsible, methodical interrogation of the lived experience of the past. But history departments still remained skeptical about whether or not we could investigate something as slippery, fleeting, and unrecorded as a historical inner experience. The discourse of historical objectivity eschewed the experiential and made it merely "personal" (Heller, 2024, p. 47). Historians continued to promote experience as "incompatible with certainty" (Agamben, 2007, p. 20). It should be noted that historians regularly characterized "historical experience" as a misleading, sentimental, "womanish" idea, more about personal investment and sentimental subjectivity than the "hard, cold fact" that was the legitimate object of inquiry (Berlant, 2008).

In the field of religion, those few historians investigating "religious experience" often limited themselves to the historical individual's claims of rapture and mystical vision. Orthodox religious institutions like monasteries were less investigated, with historians biased by secular cynicism (and Protestant critique) against "genuine" religious experience being cultivated in such places. Modern religionists thought of experience as a sincere, private, internal connection undergone by rebellious individuals like female mystics (e.g., Mechtild of Magdeburg) or countercultural hermits (e.g., Julian of Norwich or Francis of Assisi). Creedal statements recited *en masse*, doctrinal theology, or the liturgy were all more often seen as disingenuous prescriptions externally imposed top-down by the religious institution, manipulative of the devotee (Althoff, 2020). The authorities prescribing devotional practice and writing devotional scripts in society (i.e., clerics, theologians, and, most important for my research, abbots, and monks[4]) were often doubted as authentic experiencers of religion themselves, depicted as instructors more interested in controlling their audiences than feeling genuinely connected to their own ideas (Asad, 1987; Bloch, 1989). One of the clichés that burdens historians of religious experience is that passivity has been upheld as a sign of genuinely inward religious experience – this "passivity" of sincere religious devotion was particularly important to William James, who famously described religious experience as an encounter with the divine that happens *to* a subject, rather than one instigated *by* them through practice. James was speaking at the turn of the twentieth century from a Protestant tradition, one that valued "indwelling," "witnessing," and "involuntary" "enthusiasm" as God's work in the world, rather than experience actively cultivated by a devotee (Taves, 2000, pp. 9, 22–23, 352). These ideas fueled a scholarly bias against active instigations of religious experience (creedal statements, liturgies, works, etc.), turning secular historians against historical devotional practices that seemed to be constructed or cultivated by scripts (James, 2009). With such neglect, coenobitic monastic religious become cardboard cutouts in history books, and communal devotees become flat historical subjects who didn't practice what they preached. This flatness makes it easier for scholars to misconstrue these historical subjects as believers only insofar as faith served an ulterior motive, and our modern understanding of the dynamics of the historical experience of belief thus remained shallow, uncomplicated, and under-investigated (Ferrer, 2009, p. 34). This is a real problem since assertions of belief and devotional experience have played significant roles in some rather important moments in history, from the conversion of the Roman Empire to the American Civil Rights movement and beyond.

---

[4] In this Element, I will often use the word "monk" to signify medieval religious men and women, monks and nuns.

2.2 Past Attempts at Recovering Historical Experience

A handful of historians have attempted to poke the bear of "historical experience," often in subfields like "ethnohistory," the "history of emotions," the "history of the senses," and (most recently) the "history of experience" (Jarasuch, 1989; Scott, 1991; Dray, 1999; Hunt, 2009; Katajala-Peltomaa, 2022, p. 9). Early in the twentieth century, William Dilthey and R.G. Collingwood championed the search for "experience," arguing that it was able to be universally perceived. Collingwood said things like: "We understand what Newton thought by thinking it – not copies of his thoughts ... but his thoughts themselves over again. When we have done that, we know what Newton thought, not mediately, but immediately" (Collingwood, 1972; Dilthey, 2002; Schneider, 2014, p. 37). These early appeals to experience have been almost totally rejected by historians of experience today (Boddice, 2020, pp. 23–26). And they should be – for how can we be assured that if we trace the path of Newton's thoughts in 2025, we will think and understand as he himself did in his historical moment? Human thought is not universal, and our modern biases strongly obscure our seeing the past clearly.

In the 1990s, a more considered, contingent idea of "historical experience" was characterized by historian Joan Scott. Scott declared that experience was not natural or biologically determined, but was always a "linguistic event," subject to historically contingent discourses of gender, power, sexuality, and the like – in other words, not in control of the individual experiencer at all, but wholly a product of their context (Scott, 1991, p. 793). Scott moved to correct Collingwood by incorporating discourse into the realm of historical experience. Alternatively, Frank Ankersmit, Georges Didi-Huberman, and Glenn Peers each asserted that experiencing the past *was* possible in the way Collingwood imagined it, but only through nontextual, *material* remains. To them, the past remained alive in the objects, paintings, and spaces that have survived into the present (Ankersmit, 2005, p. 115; Moxey, 2013, pp. 25, 57, 117; Peers, 2024, pp. 165–199). As yet another alternative, historians began studying mirror neurons and the history of the senses, claiming that mirroring the movements of the past (e.g., walking through a medieval church) could allow historians to access the involuntary visceral feelings of historical people (Rider, 2015, p. 166; Tullet, 2022, p. 287).

But questions remain for each of these schools of thought. Carrie Noland asked of Scott, "If our agency is governed by systems of signification ... or anonymous power structures ... then why do variation, innovation, and resistance occur?" (Noland, 2009, p. 1). Jörg Rüpke moved to refine Scott's definition, claiming experience was an "aggregate of individual practices ... as well as the constraints that impinge upon these practices" – in other words, not only the discourse that trapped the individual but also the individual's shaping and making of his own life despite that/counter to that discourse (Gasparini, 2020, p. 67). Faculty members of the Research Council of Finland's Centre for Excellence in the History of Experiences,[5] Raina Toivo and Sari Katajala-Peltomaa, described the "history of experience" as a culturally bounded social process, a feedback loop that is both bottom-up (from individuals, especially non-elites) *and* top-down (from institutions, groups, publics, and cultural scripts) (Katajala-Peltomaa, 2022, p. 13).

Rob Boddice and Mark Smith have been some of the most careful thinkers about "historical experience" in light of the historiography of "objective" and "scientific" history. To them, "experience" is ideally a historical field less siloed and textually reliant than the "history of emotions," or the "history of the senses," or the discipline of history itself. They call for a field of "history of experience" that "gives us an analytical place to stand" to determine "how it felt, or how it was, to the historical actor, defined by whatever notion of the self or the subject or the collective was in play for the actor in question at the time ... the way in which living was real in historical terms" (Boddice, 2020, pp. 22, 23). They also recommend historians undergo such analysis by working in cross-disciplinary ways, such as with neuroscientists investigating emotion from a biological perspective, joining humanists and scientists together to best "explicate how (seemingly) natural kinds [of actions] are, in fact, social kinds ... how our basic and intimate experiences are constituted in part by our moral-social valuations" (Dror, 2020, p. 191).[6]

Boddice and Smith advocate for historians to be more self-examining about the ways in which their own personal experiences mediate their abilities to analyze the past. Their thoughts on this subject are the foundation from which this Element launches:

> The rejection of anything universal or biologically essential ought to be one step in removing this danger of the uncritical transference of the historian's personal and unchecked experience into the past [e.g. because I am a woman, I can understand the experiences of historical women]. But it is not in itself sufficient. There has, also, to be a conscious process of self-examination in order to understand our own politics of selection, attention, preference, exclusion, selfhood, time, and place. While we may ask *where?* and *when?* we must do so with an acknowledgment that in the process of reconstructing a period and a place we have already imposed the concepts of 'period' and

---

[5] https://research.tuni.fi/hex/.
[6] A great example of this kind of interdisciplinary work is the movement research lab of Dr. Donna Beth Ellard (English) and Dr. Barbekka Hurtt (Biological Sciences) at Denver University.

"place" on our material, such that we can view it through a particular lens of a 'there' and a 'then'. The analytical strategies we use as historians to distance ourselves from our material cannot remain invisible, perhaps because they are unavoidable. Processes of reconstruction are not neutral, even in our best efforts at allowing historical actors to speak, to sense, to feel ... historians must build an extra step into their research, in which their own apparently automatic reactions to their sources are consciously considered and cast aside from their historical analysis (Boddice, 2020, pp. 26–27).

In other words, as a medievalist, I must find a way to disable the bias that modernity has placed on my perceptive faculties. And the chief way that I propose to do this is through a rigorous method of embodiment.

2.3 What Historians Need in a History of Experience

We must build an extra step into our research, in which our own automatic reactions to our sources are consciously considered and cast aside from our historical analysis. This is the real crux of what should irk us about the persistence of "scientific" history in the academy today: that historians are not often up front about *why* they are studying what they are studying (vis à vis their personal context) and *how* their *method* of studying that particular history is filled with anachronistic and implicitly biased assumptions. It is not the *fact* that we are biased that causes me to call practitioners of "objective" and "scientific" history hypocrites – it is because we persist in *ignoring* and under-analyzing our own subject positions as scholars and insist that our hyper-secular, hyper-modern position vis à vis history is "objective."

There are certain fields of history, of course, where this kind of extra step acknowledging the subject-position of the historian is built into the very method of analysis. The most famous example is that of critical fabulation, a technique pioneered by Saidiya Hartman and employed to great effect by subsequent scholars of Black Studies who are contending both with the fragmentary nature of the archive and with the fact that the history of Black people in the United States is a history still acute, active, alive, and living in the bodies of Black historians (Hartman, 2008; Sharpe, 2016). In this field, the historian often moves seamlessly between the past and the present, between personal narrative and historical analysis, to complete a fuller picture of a historical subject. While historians should "be cautious about appropriating practices of knowing and storytelling, like Hartman's, that are formulated specifically in response to racist violence" (Chin, 2023, p. 3), we should nonetheless learn from this method of knowing the past and questioning the past's "pastness." Another alternative way of knowing and acknowledging the subject-position of the historian is espoused by Indigenous historians, such as those of the Western Apache, for whom history is "given largely in the active present tense ('Now they are arriving . . . ')" so that they can better "speak the past into being . . . summon it with words and give it dramatic form . . . [and] produce experience by forging ancestral worlds in which others can participate and readily lose themselves" (Basso, 1996, pp. 32, 33). To Western Apache historians, "the idea of compiling 'definitive accounts' is rejected out of hand as unfeasible and undesirable" because the "past lies embedded in features of the earth" which is "closely linked to the knowledge of the self, to grasping one's position in the larger scheme of things." History is outwardly acknowledged as being written for the present and specifically from the point of view (and for the identity formation) of the historian formulating the history, such that the past and the present meld so much that "sometimes it is unclear who is quoting whom" (Basso, 1996, pp. 34, 35).

In my introduction, I told you a bit about why I have been moved to write this Element: that a majority of Anglo-American historians still feel reluctant to embrace scholarship articulating medieval religious feeling. I wondered: what extra step I needed to build into my research to disarm – or at least highlight – the automatic scholarly reaction to medieval devotional writings, where cynicism and skepticism blocked the possibility that medieval religious individuals were genuinely committed to their religious goals. I needed a technique or a method that would trouble academic confidence in their own cynical perceptions of the medieval past – and one that would, of course, reveal my own biases as well. I thought about my medieval subjects compared to my modern readers, and the answer was right there: a key faculty of human experience was missing from the vast majority of scholarly investigations of historical inner experience: embodiment. Historians persist in using their disembodied intellects alone to construct knowledge of the past – even scholars of historical experience itself! Professional historians do not *DO* – instead, they think, analyze, and read (Wiles, 2003, p. 3). Even when working with neuroscientists who are observing embodied human behavior, most historians are not using their own embodiment or belief or emotion to process their data – they are relying solely on their brains, their disembodied, analytical intellects to better understand what is happening in their research.

In this way, *rational* academic historians are liable to see their objects of study as *rational* actors first and foremost – mirrors of the historians' own method of studying these objects (Schaefer, 2015, p. 16). Historians see their objects' actions as windows into past "ethical, ontological or theological assertions," *discourses* instead of "dynamic, lived, and fluidly embodied set[s] of actions, practices, gestures and speech acts," because that is how the historian's craft works in the modern academy (and has worked, in one way or another, since Ranke and the nineteenth century) (Chambers, 2013, pp. 1–2). This method is therefore less like a window to the past than a two-way mirror: historians act as if they are looking through clear glass at their subjects, when in fact their view is occluded by a reflection of themselves. We must, first of all, be honest about this presence of the historian's self, the way Hartman and the Western Apache historians are. But we should also consider whether there might be a way to look through this two-way mirror differently. We need to change the way modern historians *do* history to better align our modern *practices* with historical ones – so that our methods align a bit more with those of our objects of study and don't merely reflect our own (anachronistic) selves.

3 Why We *Should* Use Performance in Historical Inquiry

What happens, then, if historians envision what we want to know using our *bodies* as well as our intellects since the historical experiences of which we write were necessarily physical as well as mental? (Chaganti, 2023, p. 13). What happens if we place our own bodies into analytical practices in historically informed ways? Part of the reason why embodiment has not been considered by historians is that historians persist in fetishizing archival text and don't know what other materials there might be to fuel their inquiries. But part of it is also that historians are not familiar with academic fields of study like Performance Studies, fields that use embodiment as a scholarly means of analytical inquiry.

> The dominant way of knowing in the academy is that of empirical observation and critical analysis from a distanced perspective: "knowing that," and "knowing about." This is a view from above the object of inquiry: knowledge that is anchored in paradigm and secured in print. This propositional knowledge is shadowed by another way of knowing that is grounded in active, intimate, hands-on participation and personal connection: "knowing how," and "knowing who." This is a view from ground level, in the thick of things. This is knowledge that is anchored in practice and circulated within a performance community, but is ephemeral ... Since the enlightenment project of modernity, the first way of knowing has been preeminent. Marching under the banner of science and reason, it has disqualified and repressed other ways of knowing that are rooted in embodied experience, orality, and local contingencies. Between objective knowledge that is consolidated in texts, and local know-how that circulates on the ground within a community of memory and practice, there is no contest. It is the choice between science and "old wives' tales" (note how the disqualified knowledge is gendered as feminine) ... These are the nonserious ways of knowing that dominant culture neglects, excludes, represses, or simply fails to recognize ... they are illegible; they exist, by and large, as active bodies of meaning, outside of books, eluding the forces of inscription that would make them legible, and thereby legitimate ... scholarship is so skewed towards

texts that even when researchers do attend to extralinguistic human action and embodied events they construe them as texts to be read (Conquergood, 2013, pp. 33–35).

The above quotation was written by Dwight Conquergood, one of the canonical scholars of Performance Studies, a field founded in the mid-twentieth century (Schechner, 2001).[7] Performance Studies is an interdisciplinary field that has long grappled with the differences between the archive ("knowing that"; "secured in print") and the repertoire ("ephemeral" "practice"; "in the thick of things") of embodied movements, memories, and emotions often deemed unknowable by historians (Taylor, 2003). Only a small handful of historians have thought about performance at all when thinking about history – and even fewer have engaged with performance studies theories. Historian Carol Symes explains: "the use of performance as a category of analysis … takes the historian beyond the stage of strip-mining a document for facts. It enlivens the residue of human communications encoded in and manufactured by texts, reminding us that they participated in a communicative process that ancient and medieval rhetoricians called *actio*, enactment. It thereby provides a tool for the re-embodiment of the historical record and the reexamination of the causal relationship between texts and events" (Symes, 2007, pp. 14–15).

My hypothesis – which I tested in 2023–2024 while a Visiting Scholar in the Department of Performance Studies at NYU Tisch School of the Arts – is that doing embodied, historically informed, devised performance and reperformance alongside archival excavation can be helpful in propelling historians toward a clearer understanding of the past. To better understand historical experience, we as scholars must also "do it," as our historical actors did: we must supplement our training and "counter-invest in the body as a site of possibility" (Hartman, 1997, p. 51).[8] How can we historians, using "embodied cognition" ourselves (Stoller, 1997, p. xv; Mason, 2018, p. 105), *activate* the complexity of our historical subjects, instead of just inadequately describing them in history books? How does our engagement in performance, in doing, allow us to slough off our anachronistic misconceptions and open up our archival texts – and our histories – in ways we never have before?

I am advising a reperformance of historical actions – with our bodies, our voices, the historical environment, and more – in order to understand our

---

[7] Conquergood, interestingly, was trained as a medievalist (Conquergood, 2013, pp. 328–330).
[8] I quote Hartman here *not* to appropriate her work but to highlight the similarity: scholarly disruption of the field of history might often require attention to the body. In this vein, Deepesh Chakrabarty notes that there is often a similarity between premodern studies and post-colonial studies, simply because both are attacking the products and projects of modernity (Chakrabarty, 2002).

historical subjects more deeply (Auslander, 2013). As academics, we only engage in methods like performance when teaching, never really considering embodied epistemology as a rigorous historical method. Here I am recommending reperformance as a scholarly method. I am proposing singing the medieval liturgy (as Susan Boynton, Margot Fassler, and Ralph Torta do in their own work[9]); I am proposing building a castle using medieval methods (as they are doing at Guédelon[10]); I am proposing walking a medieval pilgrimage route (like historian Annette Esser mapping out a Hildegard pilgrimage[11]). Embodied history changes the way the historian approaches the text in the archive; the historian has to immerse their body in the past and feel (productively) discombobulated, pushing themselves to experience and perceive the past anew. We can discover something new about the past through participation in the "immersive conditioning" of reperformance (Gianacchi, 2011, p. 33). The process of reperformance becomes a process of "making history in dialogue,"

> co-creative, co-embodied, specially framed, contextually and intersubjectively contingent, sensuous, vital, artful in its achievement of narrative form, meaning, and ethics, and insistent on *doing through saying*: on investing the present and future with the past, re-marking history with previously excluded subjectivities, and challenging the conventional frameworks of historical knowledge with other ways of knowing (Pollack, 2005, p. 2).

It becomes an experience that is a "process which 'presses out' to an 'expression'" – it is a process of "making" history in community alongside both past and present actors (Madison, 2005, pp. 147, 167).

It is important to note that I am not proposing *theater* or *theatricality*; I am also not proposing a restaging of the past or reenactment. These verbs – *reenact* and *restage* – imply an attention to the frozen, material *facts* of the past (e.g., asking, which buttons are period-appropriate for this military uniform? Did they use beeswax candles in this city at this time?) and not always an *active investigation* or *imagination* of it. I am proposing a *reperformance* of the past – that historians, admitting the differences between 2025 and their past subjects, become participant-observers in past actions, *actively* exploring the *emotion* of the past, not merely animating its texts and material remains. There

---

[9] Susan Boynton regularly convenes a group to sing medieval Compline services on Tuesday evenings at Columbia University (Ralph Torta does something similar: https://salutemmundo.wordpress.com/2024/09/12/why-reenact-the-medieval-night-office-in-the-twenty-first-century/). Fassler modeled the way Hildegard von Bingen thought about the world in her *Scivias* by digitally modeling Hildegard's "cosmic egg" for the modern planetarium: www.medievalists.net/2015/08/hildegards-cosmos-and-its-music-making-a-digital-model-for-the-modern-planetarium/.

[10] See Rider, 2015, p. 171, and www.guedelon.fr/en/.

[11] https://litpress.org/Products/6765/The-Hildegard-of-Bingen-Pilgrimage-Book.

is a significant difference between theater/reenactment and performance as I am using it here.[12] Along with many scholars of contemporary performance, I think of theater in its modern iteration as 'playing pretend' on a proscenium stage, the audience passive, silent, and in the dark; reenactment often reads as theatrical impersonation, something persuasive but ultimately mimetic and not exploratory (Enders, 1992, pp. 21–22). The prizing of perfected naturalism in modern theater – of 'method' acting – has caused modern viewers to elide the word "performance" with "theatrical," using both words to mean something artificial, representative but illusory (Dox, 2004; Dox, 2016). As a result, we often colloquially use the word "performance" to mean faked or feigned – for example, he was "performing" the duties of a good son (but not really feeling committed to them); she was "over-performing" as a gracious hostess (and it felt disingenuous). Therefore, my using the word "performance" might at first glance feel, to a twenty-first-century scholar who is *not* a scholar of performance already, as the *opposite* of "true" history (Farrugia, 2024, p. 443).

But the performance methodology I'm proposing is different from impersonation or reenactment. I am intentionally using the term *reperformance* because, as anthropologist Tim Ingold describes, reperformance means, "a way of knowing *from the inside* … To practice this method is not to describe the world, or to represent it, but to open up our perception to what is going on there so that we, in turn, can respond to it" (Ingold, 2013, pp. 5, 7). The performance artist Marina Abramovic also makes this distinction, saying: "*Theatre* is fake: there is a black box, you pay for a ticket, you sit in the dark and see somebody playing somebody else's life. The knife is not real, the blood is not real, and the emotions are not real. *Performance* is just the opposite: the knife is real, the blood is real, and the emotions are real" (Schneider, 2014, p. 71). Reperformance in this Element is thus not a proposal for a battle reenactment with period weapons, old-timey accents, and a passive audience of tourists watching on the sidelines, nor is it a theatrical restaging of old texts. Instead, it solicits the active, earnest participation of the historian, inviting the historian to use "embodiment as an epistemic space" (Gordon, 1997, p. 13; Spatz, 2020, p. 3), allowing their "kinesthetic imagination" to become activated so that new scholarly knowledge can be created (Roach, 1996, p. 26). A historian reperforms Civil War history when he wears 2025 clothes but uses the techniques of Civil War medics to dress a wound; or marches along the routes of a traveling army to begin to better understand what it was to be

---

[12] There is also a distinction between "reperformance" as I see it here and "participant-observation." Participant-observation comes from Anthropology, and tends to signify participation in a living culture. By invoking "reperformance," I am acknowledging that a kind of revival is happening – a revival from a culture that no longer performs (or lives) as it once did.

a member of a troop in deployment; when he fully invests his body and emotion into the space in between the lines of a scholarly source.[13] If the historian performs a certain motion repeatedly, by making an antiquated craft, or doing a historical religious ritual, "his own body will eventually be inscribed, the muscles and ligaments physiologically altered, by the gestural routine that expresses and confines his body at the very same time." With such inscription, historians can begin to develop their own "kinesthetic sensation" as part of their arsenal of historical approaches and methods, allowing them "to judge the accuracy of other knowledges and beliefs." (Noland, 2009, p. 1). Historians and scholars so often dismiss such embodied sensation as lesser than intellectual judgment; but Carrie Noland notes that "only an academic prejudice could incline us to disregard bodily sensations because they have, supposedly, been constructed by discourse; only an academic prejudice could incite us to consider the material body to be abject and foreclosed" (Noland, 2009, p. 13). When we invite bodily sensation to be a part of the historian's toolbox and use it to open up our readings of the past, we start doing fresh, innovative history, stripped of some of our modern biases and the blinders imposed by professional training.[14]

What reperformance emphasizes to the historian is the messy process of creation that was involved in any historical event. When we look at deposited archival sources, or at cathedrals, or at published edicts or laws, we are more often than not looking at finished products, which can then easily be analyzed as "indexical of the social milieu and cultural values of its makers," carriers of discourse and the like (Ingold, 2013, pp. 7, 41). Reperformances of historical actions (of the scribing *practice* that made the archival records, or the *process* of the building of the cathedral, or the *debates* that yielded the edicts and laws) allow historians to actively "think *through* observation rather than *after* it" (Ingold, 2013, p. 11). By *doing* historical actions with their bodies, historians can "conjure" and make visible the liveliness and newness of historical events, seeing practice as not perceived or conceived, but as *process*. Simultaneously, *doing* history leads historians to better understand both their *own* subject positions as historians and the subject positions of their historical objects (Gordon, 1997, p. 13). Rebecca Schneider further clarifies:

> To read "history" . . . as a set of sedimented acts [is] the act of securing any incident backwards . . . This is not to say . . . that past events didn't happen . . . [Rather, we should] resituate the site of any knowing of history as body-to-body

---

[13] Young adult non-fiction writer and historian Steve Sheinkin, for instance, retraced the Vrba-Wetzler escape from Auschwitz-Birkenau to Slovakia: www.hbook.com/story/the-writers-page-walking-in-their-footsteps-an-impossible-escape-research-trip.

[14] Michael Baxandall calls this the "period eye" – what I'm describing is a kind of "period body" – eyes, nose, mouth, knees, hands, heart, and so on (Baxandall, 1988, p. 29).

transmission ... we [should] refigure "history" onto bodies, the affective transmissions of showing and telling (Schneider, 2011, p. 104).

The invitation for a historian to embody historical sources is an acknowledgment that history was not static when it was lived; it was not calcified and memorialized as a clear milieu or discourse. Instead, it was always in the "very process of becoming" (Bakhtin, 2021, p. 23). Reperformance is thus a more accurate translation of the past for the historian; it does not merely imitate or describe past behaviors, it restores them as *behaviors being made* (Schechner, 1985; Brook, 1995, p. 139). The archives can tell us of the technique – the sets of rules for a historical liturgical performance, for instance – but what happens if the historian *practices* that liturgy, instead of just reading the rules? (Spatz, 2015, pp. 40–44). Medieval drama scholar Elizabeth Dutton explains:

> The choices that a modern researcher [makes] may or may not be the same as those medieval practitioners made – usually it is impossible to know – but performance research can engage with material effects in the same way as did medieval practitioners, for the laws of the material world do not change ... Research performances are perhaps, at best, "blue sky thinking," and they are experiments that require humanities scholars to engage with volatile elements that are far less fixed than the printed page (Dutton, 2019, pp. 253, 259).

Through reperformance, historians can gain a new style of interpretation, one that does not "excavate" or "dig 'behind,'" but rather one that "takes sensory experience" and past actions seriously, no matter how unmodern past subjects might seem (Sontag, 1966, pp. 4–5).[15] Reperformance activates not *the* definitive history of a past event, but *a* history of that event – it opens up the possibilities. An increased awareness replaces a need for certainty on the part of the historian.

"Making" and "doing" as a historical method have been engaged by only a handful of historians and historiographies thus far. (Many historians might do this kind of work in their classroom teaching[16], but again, I am here emphasizing that this bodily epistemology is not just pedagogical but should be used in *scholarly research*.) The most prominent example is Pamela Smith, a historian of early modern science, whose "Making and Knowing Project" at Columbia[17] has questioned how historians analyze the history of science: "History of

---

[15] Sensory experience and epistemology, of course, has been taken seriously by people in dance, movement, and bodywork for hundreds of years. People like Bonnie Bainbridge Cohen, Moshe Feldenkrais, Marcel Mauss, and even Thich Nhat Hahn have long believed in the unity of mind and body, and that by listening to the body's experience through mindful feeling, sensing, and acting, one can learn just as much as by thinking (Spatz, 2015). Philosophers of belief have also long supported the idea that *doing* creates *belief* even more than *explaining* does (Buchak, 2014).

[16] For instance, in the Reacting to the Past project: https://reacting.barnard.edu.

[17] www.makingandknowing.org.

science is not a history of concepts, or at least not that alone, but a history of making and using of objects to understand the world," Smith argues. "The common view of craftspeople more or less mindlessly following a collection of recipes and rules – which are said to be fundamentally different from 'science' – has greatly distorted our understanding of the growth of natural knowledge in the early modern period" (Smith, 2017, p. 13). Knowledge, Smith argues, is acquired over time by means of the body – knowledge is, in the Bordieuan estimation, an "assemblage of embodied aptitudes and not systems of symbolic meanings" (Asad, 1997, p. 47). Too often, post-Enlightenment and post-Rankean historians who embraced discourses of power have seen historical subjects as "mindless" pawns in the game of some overwhelming force. But even the most powerless subject in history had a subjectivity that they embodied. Thus, Smith argues:

> [History] writing about craft is to take on a form of knowledge rooted in particular human capacities that is intractably difficult to articulate in words and texts. This brings us back to our repeated question – why try? Although their texts appear to give more or less transparent instructions, the artisan authors surveyed here sought both to upend a social and intellectual hierarchy and to articulate a particular way of knowing that, long before the research on embodied cognition, laid out the workings and power of this form of knowledge. One of my aims in this book is to highlight their view that intelligence is not held by the mind alone, but, instead, emerges from the work of the hand (Smith, 2022, pp. 17–18).

Smith quotes a French potter, Bernard Palissy, who wrote in 1563 that "however good a brain you may have, you will still make a thousand mistakes, which cannot be learned from writings, and even if you had them in writing, you would not believe them until practice has given you a thousand afflictions" (Smith, 2022, p. 218). As living human beings who have embodied practices ourselves (played pianos, run marathons, cooked casseroles), we know Palissy to be right – and yet, as historians, we over-trust in the "writings" that are left behind in archives. We are "scriptocentric" and make ourselves immune to the affect of "doing" so as not to bias our supposedly objective analyses (Taylor, 2003, pp. 10–11). Medievalist Mary Carruthers agrees with this, calling this scholarly scriptocentrism ridiculous when describing the "craft" of memory in the Middle Ages: "Academic practitioners in the modern university have taken to concentrating on 'scientific' subject matter ... but no craft fares well intellectually when its students find themselves only explicating its handbooks – consider how dry and pointless cooking would seem were it studied entirely in terms of the textual relationship to recipe books, and no one went near a kitchen!" (Carruthers, 2010, p. 100). In other words, by *doing* as historians, we become more aware of "what [we] *do not* know, even what [we] do not yet know how to ask" (Smith, 2022, p. 229). "Epistemological alterity" – like performance as a method for history – "dramatizes the limitations of history *as* knowledge" (Seth, 2024, p. 136). What results when the historian does this might be a bit messier than what we are used to in traditional, controlled, answer-filled historical scholarship. The strict rules of the academy do not allow for us to fully describe the unruliness of historical experience; it was, in the words of theater director Peter Brook, "immediate, holy, and rough" (Brook, 1995).

Reperforming and *doing* with one's body as a historian is also a radically democratizing and decolonizing method for our discipline, one that works to undo the historical epistemologies Western historians have held fast to for at least two hundred years. This practice ignites both the historian and their scholarly audience, transforming them all from a collection of "objective" spectators to active, vulnerable witnesses. By engaging our vulnerability, by making us take off our shoes, use our bodies, or physicalize the actions of people from the past, performance incites in us a heightened sense of the uncanniness of history: it hints at the spirit beyond the sources, the lived everyday that is not contained in words. As historians, it is our job to actively explore our subjects in different ways, forget that we're "experts" so that we might catch ourselves off-guard, disarm our knee-jerk critical reactions, and sojourn into historical investigations without the academic armor of our professional training. Reperformance allows for a "change in habitual perception" (Miller, 2012, p. 2) for historians. It topples the historian from our pedestals of knowing. It makes the historian put literal skin in the game – use our bodies to investigate hypotheses – and puts us on equal footing with our subjects of study. It reverses the traditional notion that "the 'professor' is the one who has knowledge and to whom [we] should listen" (Freire, 2000, p. 63). The vulnerability required for reperformance requires the historian to "share an intimacy with the other [the historical subject] that is sustained by an intimacy with the [scholar's] self" (Noland, 2009, p. 14). Performance disarms us, taking us out of the abstract analysis and putting us into the more vulnerable, concrete investigation: as Brecht says, "The world of knowledge takes a crazy turn /when teachers themselves are taught to learn." History fundamentally changes, and the ethics of our history suddenly become more democratic and generous to our historical subjects (Loveless, 2019, pp. 24–25).

To be clear, like most historians, I am deeply aware of the fact that an accurate recreation of the past is utterly impossible. I know that we cannot fully understand the experience of anyone from the past, no matter how alike their identities or lives were to ours in the present. I am also not proposing verisimilitude. We cannot *completely* know the past through doing. "Not only can we not reproduce the sensory and emotional signatures of a given time and place; we are simply ill-equipped to re-consume them, re-experience them in the same way that contemporaries did" (Boddice, 2020, p. 23). But I do see these reperformances as Brechtian demonstrations, argumentative provocations that point at something important in past history, with historians performing not "as" a historical character but "as if" a historical character (Bryan-Wilson, 2018, p. 28). Historians prefer the archive and the disembodied text because they provide the conceptualized illusion of a fixed and frozen past, like a scientific specimen "encased in amber" (Eire, 2023, p. 376). But reperformance demands that historians confront the humanity and active liveness of the past in order to trouble *how it is that historians claim to know it*. By bringing past actions into the present, historians can attempt to play through the past, "working it out" alongside our historical objects, not from a place of judgment or feigned imitation, but in a serious attempt to understand how history was dynamic, lived, and unfixed.

4 How Embodied Epistemology Is Particularly Suited to Studying Certain Historical Topics: The Example of Medieval Monasticism

This proposed embodied epistemology can be especially suited to certain types of history particularly. The history of religion and the history of medieval Christianity are two such types. As discussed earlier in this Element, these two fields are quite trapped and inhibited by the traditional, Rankean discourse of objective, scientific *Wissenschaft*. In this Rankean mode, medieval religious history sometimes becomes "functionally synonymous with ideology – a set of lies designed to mask certain material interests in accumulating ... 'social benefits'" (Jakobsen, 2008, pp. 2, 7). Scholars say things like "Isis was not a goddess but a strategy" (Rüpke, 2016, p. 72) or the Crusades were not a movement motivated by piety but rather by colonialism (Mitterauer, 2010). Religion in the hands of these scholars is "a linguistic move made in a multidimensional chess game played by bodies embedded within an economically arranged, zero-sum social landscape ... [a] text-like technolog[y] of social control" (Schaefer, 2015, p. 20).

Some of this skepticism toward medieval ecclesiastics is warranted. Many liturgical texts depicting monastic devotional practices were indeed written down to control and regulate performance, making it staid, formal, and boring (Symes, 2016, p. 243). Scholars like Talal Asad have done essential work to show how religious rituals need to be unpacked in order to highlight how they served as discourses of power (Asad, 1993, p. 62; Foucault, 1995, p. 137). Scholarly investigations of how emotion has been fabricated as cultural identity have been helpful in unpacking the dynamics and strategies of medieval communities (Sterk, 2014, p. 6). But we don't see how medieval monastic performances "efficaciously transmitted collective memories, values, and belief systems" by dynamically engaging the audience in a relational, communal way (Taylor, 2003, pp. 40, 69). We cannot feel the qualities of monastic inner experience divorced from their discursive meaning. Historians often miss how the world created by medieval monastic performance was one of shared imagination and experience (Turner, 1982, pp. 7–60; Bissell, 2018, p. 2; Page, 2021, p. 5). We have no video recordings or oral histories from medieval monks; we have no newspapers; we have no *proof* of devotional or emotional experience. In the words of Carlos Eire:

> When all is said and done, phenomena deemed impossible in the twenty-first century remain a risky liminal field of study, suspended between legitimacy and illegitimacy. Rooted as they are in belief and closely tied as they are to a worldview directly derived from ancient and material times, these phenomena are markers of alterity; that is, they reify a premodern "otherness" that is at once marginal, primitive, and somewhat unsettling to many in modern society who ... prefer to keep the supernatural safely encased in amber (Eire, 2023, p. 376).

This *a priori* pessimistic scholarly approach to monastic devotion as barely knowable, or as solely a discourse of power, is a major roadblock (Schaefer, 2015, p. 16). It disables our trust in our own perception that could further uncover the monastic past (Morgan, 2009, p. 10). Just as archival absences are felt keenly by historians, the blind spots of medievalists also produce absence and loss (Fricke, 2022, p. 6). A partial solution to this issue, however, might lie in the engaged knowledge that comes from historical reperformance: scholarly cynicism can be momentarily disengaged when the historian can be fully taken in by their own act and learn to believe in the historical experiences they are reperforming (Goffman, 1959, pp. 17–24).

4.1 Medieval Monastic Epistemology Was Itself Embodied

In medieval historical practice, devotion was *not* a text-only experience; rather, it was an "embodied epistemology" (Morgan, 2009, p. 9). Medieval monastic life is peppered with liturgical ritual – monks attend the church services of the monastic office eight times a day; they sing through all 150 psalms once every week; and they celebrate the Eucharist at mass (a.k.a. communion, when they believe they eat the body and drink the blood of Jesus) at least once a day. Moreover, monastic life was in its totality a durational performance: every moment experienced by monastic bodies was considered and regulated, down to the food they ate, the clothes they wore, and the direction they lay their heads when they slept.

In order to get at monastic religious experience, then, historians explore the extra-textual ways of understanding that medieval monastics used. In some liturgical performances, monks' bodies were used for mimesis, imitating the biblical past so that medieval Christians could experience it bodily, more easily applying its salvific benefits to themselves (Yardley, 2006, p. 152). For example, on Maundy Thursday, Christian abbots washed their monks' feet, imitating the example of Jesus washing the feet of his disciples in the Gospels. In this way, the events of the Last Supper on Holy Thursday were reenacted by medieval monks, but the idea that even the most advanced officers in the monastery should humble themselves in this way was viscerally understood through embodied participation. Such role-playing helped participants to better understand, but also to experience in their bodies, the emotional contours of the dynamics between apostles and Jesus, allowing devotees to experience the religious feelings of these events that they had read about in texts so many times before (Yardley, 2006, p. 143; Swift, 2011). Occasionally, such performances did not use live performers to enact such dramas, as in the case of the Church of Saint Eulalia in Catalonia, where Christians would wander between jointed and manipulatable life-size Romanesque sculptures of biblical characters during the Crucifixion (Figure 1; Weigert, 2015, pp. 7, 26, 45–46).

Figure 1 From the twelfth-century church of Saint Eulalia in Erill la Vall, Catalonia, now in the Museu Episcopal de Vic. MEV, Museu d'Art Medieval. Photographer: Salvans.

The sculptures offered a tactility that would stir the soul's desire not through text, but through an active physicality. Of course, this tactile sensation was a paradox: here, devotees had the opportunity to physically grasp a wooden Christ, to feel materially connected to God, when they simultaneously knew intellectually that God was the most elusive and least graspable being in their conception – a painful knowledge which all monks shared. Embodied events like these were occasions to remember that active embodiment was what would determine an audience member's salvation, not disembodied contemplation. Medieval monastic devotion was thus performative not in the sense of inauthentic, but in the sense of a performative speech-act: the doing made it so (Austin, 1975). Monasticism was a space ignited by experience as much as it was by book learning – it was, at its essence, "a shared imaginary" experienced through text, sound, movement, space, smells, tastes, and touch – sensations which historians rarely engage *themselves* when analyzing the monastic past (Morgan, 2009, p. 7).

So if historians want to understand monks at all – what they did, why they did it, how they felt when they were doing it, and how their belief systems were affected by doing what they did – we need to change the ways historians explore this history, going beyond textual evidence and resuscitating the traces of embodied experience cultivated by medieval monastic ritual.[18] We need to use performance and reperformance to *do* history. The method I am proposing is *particularly* appropriate for the medieval period since it is the epistemological method embraced by medieval monks. This participatory restored behavior was fundamental to the way that monks understood their religion. The eleventh-century monk Peter of Celle noted that this way of knowing was especially monastic and was often neglected and ignored by *medieval* academics in the universities that were new in the Central Middle Ages:

> To inquire after oneself in God and God in Himself is indeed one great question. Actually, another inquiry precedes it, to seek oneself in oneself [*se in se quaerere*], which far reaching inquiry ... is opened up through the mastery of the *flesh* ... This inquiry is rarely undertaken by *academics in the schools of cities and towns*. Since it is hardly ever urged there, it is more rarely completed. They pay less attention to this one question, when they are involved in as many unnecessary as necessary ones and a crowd of people even forcefully urges the *facile and chattering disputants to solve questions which have been raised*. By contrast, our solitary inquiry goes better in

---

[18] My first plea to historians to this effect was in the American Historical Association's trade magazine, *Perspectives on History*, in April 2024: www.historians.org/perspectives-article/embodied-knowledge-lessons-from-my-seven-year-old-daughter-april-2024/.

silence and is more perfectly studied in solitude. It is of the *heart,* not the *mouth* (Peter of Celle, 1987, pp. 139–140).

One could argue that the "facile and chattering" disembodiment Peter witnessed in the eleventh-century proto-universities is most fully realized in the methodologies of "scientific" historical empiricism of history departments in the twentieth century.[19] Peter emphasizes that such disembodiment is far from the medieval *monastic* understanding of devotional investigation, for medieval monks saw Christian knowledge and Christian theology as a fundamentally embodied practice ("of the flesh" and the "heart"). Jesus Christ himself had taken the incarnate form of a human being; monks regularly ingested Christ's body in the form of the sacrament of the Eucharist. It was thus not through language but through em*bodied* dramatic action that Christ was best understood (Bynum, 2017). When Bernard of Clairvaux discussed devotion, faith, and conversion, he argued that "you do not need to look them up in the pages of a book. Look to experience instead" (Bernard of Clairvaux, 1987, p. 85). Christian community was physical and performed, neither assimilable to a text nor derivable from it (Beckwith, 2001).

So why do historians neglect to use their bodies in their analysis of medieval monasticism? For medievalists, any aversion to performance is actually fundamentally (ironically) *modern* and *anachronistic*. Mike Chin goes so far as to say that it is precisely traditional fields like medieval history and Classics that need "new forms of imagination … as a corrective" (Chin, 2023, p. 3). So what happens when we re-embrace the embodied epistemology of our premodern subjects and seek our subjects of inquiry much as they did, with our contemporary bodies? What can we learn as medieval historians, and what can we learn as historians more generally?

4.2 Historians Can Learn from Medieval Nonlinear Historical Time

The ceremonies of the monastery show us how the medieval monastery was an environment of a living past akin to that described by Hartman and the Western Apache historians: "the bridges between 'was', 'is', and 'will be' were stronger

---

[19] In the Middle Ages, "*experientia*" and "*experimentum*" were words that meant the same thing – an experienced experiment – whereas by the Enlightenment, "experience" signified an *in*expert, casual, unsophisticated way of knowing and "experiment" signified an objective, scientific process. Along these lines, choreographer and dancer Bill T. Jones says: "In western culture the rational, well-contained mind is considered superior to the messy, physical body. The mature developed psyche – critical moral intelligent – takes precedence over the runny nose, flailing arms, and flatulent viscera that it sits above. The body is seen as primitive compared to the highly complex brain" (Garbes, 2022, p. 153).

in the Middle Ages than at other times in European history" (Constable, 1990, p. 49). From the earliest days of medieval Christianity, theologians recommended that the events of Christ's life "should not be remembered as something past but honored as something present" (Constable, 1990, p. 51). Twelfth-century monks like William of Newburgh explained: "just as the soul of one meditating at one time reflects upon acts without observing the temporal order, moving fortuitously now from this to that, now from that to this, by the impetus of the spirit; likewise . . . with little regard for temporal order, matters of diverse times and circumstances are sung . . . with extraordinary neglect of time . . . " (as quoted in Fulton, 1996, p. 102). Embodied practices like the Eucharist were practices of performative time travel (Pickup, 2015): they were, for the monks, historical investigation and present contemplation, both. Devout monks would regularly be described as wandering around the monastery, using spaces, sculptures, and silence as vehicles for their quest to envision and witness the past events of the Bible in their present time (Chazelle, 2007, pp. 91–94; Noble, 2009, p. 311; Dinshaw, 2012, p. 18; Gertsman, 2015, p. 165; Kitzinger, 2019, pp. 3, 18, 45–46).

As historians, we have been trained to think by the Enlightenment, which describes time as linear, progressive, and always forward-moving (Dinshaw, 2012, pp. 14–15; Davis, 2017; Burrus, 2018, p. 135). Part of why we believe we can do 'objective' history is that the Enlightenment has taught us that, as historians, we have distance from the past and that the past is a finished object we can study. But the very conception of historical time as linear is historically constructed. To the Christian theologian Augustine of Hippo, history was a living past, and understanding it required "*distentio*" – a way of reaching into the past and experiencing past and future in a present time (Adler, 2022, pp. 7–10). Participant observation and embodied doing by contemporary historians of medieval monastic activities thus would also account for time in a more medieval way: according to Augustine, the present revealed and contained past action, and 'doing' would revive the past and bring it into the present and the future. This sliding temporality is incredibly premodern, as it is also quite post-modern – the ninth-century Amalarius of Metz and twelfth-century Honorius of Autun each sound like post-colonial theorist Homi Bhabha when they talk about the "time lag" created by monastic performance and liturgy (as quoted in Hardison, 1965, pp. 30–40; Biddick, 1998, p. 226). In contrast, Enlightenment notions of linear time that many academic historians insist on make our history stagnant, especially our history of the premodern world. The straightjacket of linear time was even clear to religionist William James, who noted that "when we conceptualize, we cut out and fix, and exclude anything but what we have fixed. A concept means that-and-no-other. Conceptually, time excludes space; motion and rest exclude each other; unity excludes plurality; independence excludes relativity; 'mine' excludes 'yours'; this connection excludes that connection – and so on indefinitely." But, James yearns, "in the real concrete sensible flux of life, experiences co-penetrate each other so that it is not easy to know just what is excluded and what is not" (James, 1971, pp. 243–244).

Studying medieval monastic performance – as opposed to just monastic archival texts – is therefore particularly powerful in demonstrating how an *un-modern*, un-Enlightenment notion of time can become instrumental to historians (Ahmed, 2006, pp. 14–15). Diana Taylor notes that, to a traditional archivist, the historical event of a performance would seem to have disappeared; but actually, by redoing that performance, history *reappears* by means of its trace remains (Taylor, 2003; see also Derrida, 1998). Rebecca Schneider agrees: reperforming becomes an occasion "when something from the past is shown again . . . [making it] present" (Schneider, 2011, p. 139).

The irony of historians' clinging to linear chronology is that every historian knows that the "past is not dead – in fact, it's not even past."[20] The relationship between history and memory is a regular subject of study for historians, who, in fields like the American Civil War, for instance, would absolutely acknowledge that "all history is modern history" (Schneider, 2011, p. 11). In post-colonial studies and Black Studies especially, academic historians are loosening their hold on linear time, learning to acknowledge that colonial exploitation, chattel slavery, and other horrors of the "past" are events that are "still ongoing" (Sharpe, 2016, p. 26). In the words of Suzan-Lori Parks, "History is time that won't quit" (Jucan, 2018). Gilles Deleuze notes that history *co-exists* with the present in a way unacknowledged by historians, who are often blind to how this works: "[Time] implies between successive presents non-localisable connections, actions at a distance, systems of replay, resonance and echoes, objective chances, signs, signals, and roles which transcend spatial locations and temporal successions . . . In short, what we live empirically as a succession of different presents . . . is also *the ever-increasing coexistence of levels of the past*" (Deleuze, 1995, pp. 82–83).

With this wind at my back, I want to insist that the reperformance I am proposing, then, is not as anachronistic and ahistorical as it might appear to be, especially for premodern subjects. I am not arguing that we will all have a universal experience of historical texts once they are enacted and embodied, and I am not suggesting we will "transcend history," but rather "that we transgress history, at least, our linear conception of it" (Schneider, 2011, p. 11). If academic

---

[20] This line comes from William Faulkner in (if you can believe it) his book *Requiem for a Nun*.

historians know that history is un-fixed for all histories, not just certain ones, it can be a condition that we as historians could use to our epistemological advantage. Monks themselves – in the Middle Ages, today, and throughout history – reperform the same medieval behaviors over and over again. When they enact the Maundy Thursday ritual, they revel in a notion of simultaneity, both with Christian communities in the present around the world and with the Christian communities of the past. Monasticism in this way operates like the indigenous histories of the Western Apache more than it does the modern, physical, historical archive: through repetition, monks participate in past history that is made present *by their embodied behavior* (Soussloff, 2000, p. 75). In the silence that is required to dominate monasteries, language is insufficient to capture embodiment and practice, and even unwelcome (Spatz, 2020, p. 35); instead, kinesthetic empathy is relied upon as the fundamental epistemology.

Performance, then, eschews the "prescriptive" nature of "continuous, secular," irreversible historical time (Hammann, 2016, pp. 261–262). By inverting the modern temporality through performance, however, we can privilege the "eternal" as opposed to the "temporary and contingent," which ends up being more fundamentally premodern anyway (Buck-Morss, 2021, p. 212). If our goal is "not simply [to] *describe* the complexity of a work's workings, but to *activate* its modalities of thought, its rhythms" (Massumi, 2014, p. ix), we must trouble our temporal notions as historians, as well as our methodologies. We must allow for the walls of past vs. present vs. future and the fear of anachronism to tumble around us, disengaging those critiques so that we can better enter into a state of embodied perception.

Reperformance, then, does two things: (1) it revives un-modern, vestigial, and antiquated means of knowledge – kinesthetic empathy and embodied epistemology – and adds them to the historian's toolkit, and (2) it exposes how anachronistic modern historians' linear sense of temporality is, and by troubling the idea that the past is even past, questions whether objective distance is ever possible for a historian. In these ways, reperformance is not only a practice for historians of non-western European history to engage with – it is also an essential practice for historians of medieval Europe to use. With this conviction, we will now turn to our last section, where I will show how I have used reperformance in my historical investigation of medieval monastic devotion.

5 How Can We Use Performance? The Case of Performance-Lectures in The Met Cloisters

For a few months in 2023–2024, I tried my hand at testing this hypothesis of mine by giving what I called performance-lectures at The Met Cloisters in

New York City to different local academic audiences. The Met Cloisters is an atmospheric museum which was opened in 1938 and which integrates pieces of medieval buildings into its walls, housing medieval European and Mediterranean art in a reconstituted conglomerate of real medieval architectural spaces.[21] In this way, The Met Cloisters aims to both reconstitute and simulate real medieval spatial contexts for the art it exhibits – and for this reason, I thought it an appropriate space for embodied epistemology through reperformance.[22]

Upon arriving at the museum, participants in these performance-lectures were given performance scores modeled after those scripts disseminated by Fluxus performance artists like Yoko Ono (Ono, 2000). The texts of the performance scores all came from eleventh- and twelfth-century monastic sources, how-to manuals called "customaries," which described for medieval monks what their ideal behavior should be. Using the actions described by these customaries, the scores invited participants, when encountering the art of The Met Cloisters, to perform as monastic surrogates, doing the behaviors that medieval monks would do. At the top of each event, I posited that such reperformance recovered small pieces of what we may have lost of the medieval past, pieces not found in archival text but in practiced repertoire (Schneider, 2011, p. 102). The participants and I co-performed these scores for 45 minutes together, and then, at the end of the performance part of the event, we all came together to discuss what we had found in the doing of the activities in the performance score.[23]

In the Section 5.1, I will provide full details of what we did during these performance-lectures and what we found in doing so. The event was labeled as part "lecture" – that is, something academics would recognize, an academic event featuring my new work. But the "performance" part of the title indicated that this academic lecture would not feature normal academic behavior; and indeed it didn't, requiring the audience to show, do, and participate in reperformance, which is atypical for an academic event. I chose the form of the performance-lecture to use practice and embodiment to attempt to loosen the scholar's grip on objectivity and to open up what might be knowable about the past to historians.

---

[21] www.metmuseum.org/plan-your-visit/met-cloisters.
[22] Museums have been theorized as sites for re-experiencing the past elsewhere. Recent work on this is *The Museum as Experience: Learning, Connection, and Shared Space* (Shifrin, 2023).
[23] This effort is akin to processes of co-creation that are being thought about by a new generation of museum curators and gallerists: https://tfd.kunstinstituutmelly.nl/chapbook/. I am grateful to Araceli Bremauntz-Enriquez and Miller Schulman for this citation.

As the headlining "lecturer," I did not speak more than everyone else; rather, I curated the performance score, implementing a program in which I used participants' bodies alongside my own to "intertwine imagination, memory, sensorial perception and actuality" (Fabião, 2006, pp. 123–125). At the end of the event, when we all came together in discussion, the audience members and I co-created knowledge based on what we all had done. The difference between this knowledge and the kind usually produced at an academic lecture was that ours was created in community, not delivered only in one direction from me to them. Throughout the process of this academic event, we "lock[ed] production and reception together as accomplices into one relationship ... both sides tak[ing] part simultaneously ... in the production of sense and knowledge" (Husemann, 2004, p. 4). By repeating and restoring past behavior, we all translated a piece of historical experience that was not in the archive and could only be restored through repetition, not *as* monks, but *as if* we were monks (Schechner, 2001, p. 362). By involving the body and thereby affect in our inquiry, we did not become monks, but got the feel of monasticism. And by using performance to disarm scholarly cynicism and take over our bodies, we aimed to "articulate ... the breach" (Massumi, 2014, p. viii), not "playing at being a monk" (Irvine, 2010, p. 221) but restoring monastic affective action in order to reevaluate what we think historians know about medieval monasticism. These performance-lectures thus became both "a way of knowing and a way of showing" (Kemp, 1998, p. 116). This is something that is very much a part of the form of performance-lectures more generally, practices embraced by modern and post-modern artists to comment on the art market, or the objectification of the artist, or the inanity of art criticism, among other things (Frank, 2013, p. 7).

5.1 Describing the *Ordo Monachorum* Performance-Lectures at The Met Cloisters

Over the course of six months, five different groups came to The Met Cloisters to participate in these performance-lectures. Each group was from an academic institution in New York City – two private universities, two public universities, and one private seminary. Each group had twenty-five participants, most of whom were graduate students, professors, or professional academics, but some of whom were undergraduates or members of the general public. The groups included audiences from Religious Studies, Medieval Studies, Art History, Performance Studies, Music, English/Comparative Literature, and History programs, and a Christian seminary.

Embodied Epistemology as Historical Method 31

Figure 2 First stop, in the twelfth-century Notre-Dame-de-Pontault chapter house. Photo credit: Adam Gidwitz.

Upon entering the museum (Figure 2), participants were welcomed into the twelfth-century chapter house from Notre-Dame-de-Pontault in France, and invited to clean their hands and take a performance score to keep on their laps. As they waited for each other to settle in, they were allowed to read preparatory materials in the performance score, materials which assured them – in the language of the medieval sources – that medieval people thought that merely *doing* monastic actions made someone a monk.[24] These preparatory materials also introduced them to their first bit of monastic sign language, giving them something to do with their bodies as they settled into the activities in front of them. In the medieval monastery, because silence was kept most of the time, Benedictine monks developed a system of sign language so that they could communicate and still maintain the silence (Bruce, 2007). So the opening sign instructed by the performance score that they performed as they waited for their colleagues to settle in was the sign for "hearing" ("hold your finger against your ear," Bruce, 2007, p. 181).

I then explained that, for the next forty-five minutes, a tiny fraction of the time that medieval monks practiced them, I was going to invite everyone to

---

[24] "For whether he subscribes or does not, if he strives to fulfill what the monastic order demands, he will certainly be a monk" (Constable, 2008, p. 65).

engage in a series of embodied actions that would help us explore – beyond language and text – the quality of the religious, emotional commitments of medieval monks from the twelfth century. I told them that their performance score, and my voice, were to be their only guides; they should enter into a great monastic silence and a reflective interior state, and they should not communicate with other human beings. When they heard a hand bell, they would be moving to a new part of the museum, physically following my body toward whatever galleries I led them. After about forty-five minutes, I assured them, the exercise would be over, and I would invite their feedback about the experience, to see what they might have learned about medieval monastic experience from doing. Then I opened the main performance exercises by saying:

> For the next forty-five minutes, I ask that you regulate your desire to utter words and to do things that are not part of the new discipline that I am creating; I ask that you fully commit your "inner and outer order to this new way of life" (Bruce, 2007, p. 17).
>
> Turn off the impulse to control or own the material. Listen and see what already exists, instead of trying to manipulate a material into something that looks like art or theater or dance to you. Simply be there in it, be aware and be curious. This may be uncomfortable at first. It may also be a great relief... Your learning will accumulate naturally without an objective and you will be in conversations that can lead you somewhere (Overlie, 2016, pp. 3–4).
>
> I'm going to ask that you remove anything that you might be wearing that tethers you to 2024, and to your curated presence in 2024. It might be your earrings, or your scarf, or your watch. Whatever it is, remove it, "stuff your ego and ambition into [it]" and then close your eyes and take a deep breath (Overlie, 2016, p. 4).
>
> "Since we are placed in the midst of snares [*I said holding up my own iPhone*], we easily grow cold in our heavenly longing" (John of Fécamp, 1946, p. 182). Close your eyes. Draw your right hand from your sleeve and place it upon your chest, in the sign for confession (Bruce, 2007, p. 90). I ask you each to drop your cell phone into this basket as you repeat after me: "I long to be emptied of my self" (Bernard, 1987, p. 195).

After all participants surrendered their phones and incanted, "I long to be emptied of my self," I walked participants silently to their first stop (Figure 3): the twelfth-century cloister from the Catalan monastery of Saint-Michel-de-Cuxa. (You can follow along in the performance score, available online at www.cambridge.org/HOES_Mancia.) This first station was a cloister that served as the open-air central quadrangle of the monastery and also served as a container for the garden at its center, which was both symbolic of the

Figure 3 Second stop, in the twelfth-century cloister from Saint-Michel-de-Cuxa. Photo credit: Adam Gidwitz.

Garden of Eden (paradise, heaven, the ultimate goal of monastic prayer) and a practical space (a garden filled with edible, useful, medicinal plants) for a self-sufficient institution. This stop encouraged participants to be emptied of themselves using the medieval words that monks contemplated while looking at cloisters to further "blaze up" their "lukewarmness," preparing themselves for the work of meditation (Anselm, 1975, p. 116). The stop, which lasted ten minutes in silence, aimed to mentally prepare participants for the embodied work that was about to happen. The piece of medieval monastic sign language that accompanied this station was the sign for 'not knowing' ("wipe your lips with a raised finger," Bruce, 2007, p. 181). By the last four minutes of the Cuxa stop, participants were repeating this physicalized sign (*not knowing; not knowing; not knowing*) as they waited for my handbell to ring.

We all then walked to our next station (Figure 4), where the meat of the performance-lecture began: an acknowledgment of the difficulty of these rituals. We entered the gallery built around a twelfth-century apse from San Martín in Fuentadueña, which also features a twelfth-century fresco from San Joan de Tredos (Lleida, Spain) and a twelfth-century crucifix likely from the convent of Santa Clara at Astudillo. Medieval monks understood that there would never be linear progress or consistent ascent in prayer, even for the most practiced of monks (Mancia, 2023).

Figure 4 Third stop, in the twelfth-century apse from Saint Martín in Fuentidueña. Photo credit: Adam Gidwitz.

So during the walk to this station, the score used monastic language to acknowledge the discomfort participants might be feeling entering into this practice: "How far you are from me!" the score exclaims. "I cannot see you ... I cannot come to you ... I have no experience of you" (Anselm, 1975, p. 258). As monks did in their medieval lives, the score continuously acknowledged the discomfort likely going on in the participants' minds – a parallel with the self-doubt medieval monks themselves felt and acknowledged 1,000 years ago. The boredom, transgression, and inability to "feel it" that participants experienced were therefore part of the experience of the performance lecture, as it was relevant to how medieval monks felt, too. So the idea of rituals being awkward sometimes was practiced in the performance-lecture: that "rituals do not need to feel coherent with our ideals or natural in bodies in order to be effective" was part of the point (Logan, 2022, p. 20).

The main work of this second station was to engage the body even if the participant wasn't 'feeling it'. At this station, participants were asked to prostrate themselves in the gallery space somewhere (Figure 5), to attempt to cultivate a monk-like humility: "As long as you continue to fail to shake yourself free of your own superiority, then you know quite well that you are not really humble" (William of St. Thierry, 1970, p. 135). For academics who might be self-conscious at this moment, the score reminded participants of their interconnectivity during this embodied performance: "We are members of one another" (Newman, 2021, p. 1). But it also admitted that not wanting to be there was okay, and that all one really had to do was "recognize the state in which you are" in order to do the work, which was, admittedly, awkward.

With the ring of a bell, we then moved to our third station (Figure 6): the twelfth-century chapel from Notre-Dame-du-Bourg at Langon. Here, the score

Figure 5 Third stop, in the twelfth-century apse from Saint Martín in Fuentidueña. Photo credit: Adam Gidwitz.

Figure 6 Fourth stop, in the twelfth-century chapel from Notre-Dame-de-Bourg at Langon. Photo credit: Adam Gidwitz.

invited us to sing together in the barrel-vaulted space, following the instructions of a medieval text to sing songs to the sculpted images of the Virgin Mary (Kerr, 2009, p. 55). As untrained singers, we used a medieval-inspired chanting technique coined by post-modern musician Pauline Oliveros:[25]

> *Inhale deeply. Exhale on the note of your choice, singing* "Lux." *[Latin for 'light']* Listen to the sounds around you and match your next note to one of them. On your next breath, repeat. On your next breath, be silent. Listen.[26]

You can hear what this sounded like on the online platform for this Element (Video 1).

Video 1 Fourth stop, video of the singing in Langon. Video credit: Adam Gidwitz. Video files available at www.cambridge.org/HOES_Mancia.

Our fourth stop took us from singing praises to Mary to mourning alongside her with a fourteenth-century pietà from the German Rhineland

---

[25] This follows Oliveros' "Tuning Meditation," which was even performed at The Met Cloisters: www.youtube.com/watch?v=g5bj8sO2-WY.
[26] Any italicized words in the performance scores were noted as modern additions; unitalicized text was medieval quotation.

Embodied Epistemology as Historical Method

Figure 7 Fifth stop, in front of the fifteenth-century Spanish lamentation scene. Photo credit: Adam Gidwitz.

(Figure 7). Here I paired twelfth-century monastic devotions with an admittedly later medieval sculpture (since I was constrained by the art available in the museum). Each person's score had attached to its back a piece of sackcloth, which I invited participants to use as a "*sudarium*" – sweat cloth – to mime wiping the blood, sweat, dirt, and tears off the statue in front of them (of course, they were asked not to *literally* touch the statues due to museum protocols, though medieval people actually would have).[27] When they were done wiping the sculptures, participants then

---

[27] The artificiality of the museum gallery space – and the constraints placed therein which interfere with our perception of the art – is discussed in *Inside the White Cube: The Ideology of the Gallery Space* (O'Doherty, 1976).

Video 2 Fifth stop, video in front of the fifteenth-century lamentation and fourteenth-century Pietà. Video credit: Adam Gidwitz. Video files available at www.cambridge.org/HOES_Mancia.

wiped the sweat from their own brows and then squeezed the blood, sweat, dirt, and tears from their *sudarium* into their mouths. This action was inspired by the actions listed in a collection of hagiographic miracle stories from the twelfth century (Newman, 2020, p. 141), and this station was the one that tended to absorb participants the most in imagined action. (You can watch the video of these performances in Video 2.) Still, acknowledging the need for the suspension of disbelief to perform those actions in 2024, the score again admitted that doubts might be creeping in at this point, inviting the participants to "recognize the state in which [they were]," as they had at an earlier stop too (Aelred, 1971, p. 75).

Video 3 Sixth stop, performing the sign for "Alleluia." Video credit: Adam Gidwitz. Video files available at www.cambridge.org/HOES_Mancia.

Our fifth stop (Video 3) moved us outside to the West Terrace at The Met Cloisters, which overlooks the Hudson River and the George Washington Bridge. (Ideally, this stop would have taken place inside the museum, but there is no eating in The Met Cloisters' galleries.) Here, I handed everyone a grape, and together, we read through Guigo II's eleventh-century description of how one enters into a process of meditation, prayer, and contemplation. Together, we physicalized the metaphor used by Guigo about spiritual ascent being akin to the process of chewing a grape:

> "You are a beggar, crying at the door that you have had nothing to eat today. You are so feeble you cannot open your mouth to speak." (Guigo II, 1981, p. 95) *At the same time as your colleagues, put the grape in your mouth, but do not bite it.* "This is of great sweetness, like a grape that is put into the mouth filled with many senses to feed the soul ... " *At the same time as your colleagues, bite and chew the grape.* "The soul begins to bite and chew upon this grape, as though putting it in a wine press ... Chew the honeycomb of prayerful words, suck their flavor which is sweeter than sap, swallow their wholesome sweetness. Chew by thinking, suck by understanding, swallow by rejoicing." *At the same time as your colleagues, swallow the grape* (Guigo II, 1981, p. 69).

We then all performed the sign for 'Alleluia' together, which was to "raise your hand, bend the tips of your fingers, and Move them as though flying like angels, because, as it is believed, the Alleluia is sung by the angels in heaven" (Bruce, 2007, p. 181).

Lastly, we returned once again to the Pontault Chapter House for our conclusion (Figure 8). There, we again acknowledged that many participants might not have felt satisfied or locked-in to the performance of these actions. Medieval monks didn't either, the scores assure them one final time:

> The more your soul searches the more it thirsts ...
> as long as it is meditating, so long is it suffering ...
> the fire of longing, the desire to know [God] more fully, only increases.
> Search for truth, ask, seek, knock until you receive.
> Draw your right hand from your sleeve and place it upon your chest, in the sign for
> confession. [*Close your eyes.*]
> Hear a new language which you do not know, but are now starting to hear (William, 1970, p. 153).
> [*Remain silent until you hear the bell.*]

Figure 8 Final stop, back at the chapter house. Photo credit: Adam Gidwitz.

At the ring of the bell, we all opened our eyes. I then offered their phones back to them, and as I did, I read the words of an eleventh-century monk: "It shames and sickens me to appear in public assemblies, to enter the city, to speak with the powerful ... to be concerned with the chattering masses and to endure many such things as the world does ... free me from this malignant age ... from these tumults of causes and the manifold noise of advancings, from ... this concourse of brothers where daily I offend in many things, and give me that recess of solitude and freedom of spiritual leisure" (John of Fécamp, 1946, p. 195). And then we paused, took a few breaths, and turned to our group discussion, reflecting on what was learned during these activities.

5.2 What We Learned as Historians by Performing

I should start by saying that the performances were tremendously impactful – never have I received so many positive responses, follow-up emails, and private messages after an academic event I'd participated in or curated. From November 2023 to May 2024, I gave five of these performance-lectures. Each of them was over-subscribed and had long waiting lists. After presenting to 125 people in total, I received 10 follow-up emails from people complimenting the work; 4 graduate students wrote response papers about the event; and 3 graduate students from different institutions around NYC even asked me to serve as an outside advisor on their dissertations. There was a hunger here among these academics – especially the students – that seemed whetted by the performance-lecture events. These positive, thoughtful responses are explored in the sections below.

5.2.1 Even "Objective" Academics Are Biased Observers

"I am a militant atheist, but I really got into the spirituality of the event – it was all really unexpected" seems to have been the biggest effect of the performance-lectures.[28] The vast majority of participants seem to have been affected by the way that embodied knowing forced them to turn off their scholarly cynicism about spirituality and instead confront and acknowledge the pious dimensions that were inextricable from monastic life.

My favorite example of this was shared by a post-doctoral medievalist, a self-proclaimed feminist Catholic who studied medieval monastic women. This post-doc explained that when her performance score had directed her to perform the Cluniac monastic sign language for "telling a lie" ("place a finger inside of your lips and then draw it out again," Bruce, 2007,

---

[28] This is a real quote, emailed to me from a participant after the February performance-lecture.

p. 181), her feminist hackles were raised.[29] Why is there so much surveillance in the Catholic Church? she fumed to herself. As a kind of rebellion, she experimented with which finger she placed inside her mouth (the middle finger, so she could flip the Church the bird; her thumb, so she could bite her thumb at the patriarchal institution, etc.). But I required the participants to stay for at least five minutes with each performative motion, and by minute 3 she had exhausted her anger and started experimenting in earnest. What if, instead of sticking her finger in her mouth vertically and pulling it out, she stuck her pointer finger into her mouth horizontally, parallel with her lips? Then when she pulled her finger out of her mouth, it was as if she were pulling a banderole out of her mouth (Figure 9), a medieval speech bubble; moreover, if she kept pulling her finger out of her mouth, even alternating her right and left hands, it became a movement akin to her pulling ribbons out of her mouth like a magician – which in the Middle Ages might have read as confessional, as relieving of former mendacious speech (Carruthers, 1990, pp. 44, 161). By experimenting with the physicality of monastic sign language, this medievalist ended her time far from where she had begun: she was beginning to stop seeing sign language as a product of monastic policing and started instead seeing it as a mechanism for confessional release, allowing a monk to relieve himself of the burden of carrying his lie around. The postdoc started her performance (understandably) biased against the Catholic Church, a bias that would have seeped into her archival analyses – but she ended her performance with a newly reoriented position from which she could do different archival analyses. This does not mean that she abandoned her cynicism – it means she can now pair it with a better understanding of the emotions monks felt, too.

Inversely, contemporary contemplatives, monks, religious, and priests who attended the performance-lectures found the exercise incredibly familiar and unremarkable – almost easy. The seminary students who attended felt like the work we were doing was "normal," whereas the academics from secular departments and institutions felt the opposite. One Carmelite monk shared that "sometimes I listen to historians' presentations with wonder as my own monastic experience gives me a totally different viewpoint and perspective to understand medieval religious experience ... especially in the monasteries and anchoritic cells." I am in no way claiming that monks and nuns of the twenty-first century do identical practices to the monks and nuns of the Middle Ages, but the idea that people who follow ascetic lifestyles

---

[29] Note that in the November iteration of these performance-lectures, this sign language was contained in the performance score; it was cut for the final iteration of the performance score, available online at www.cambridge.org/HOES_Mancia.

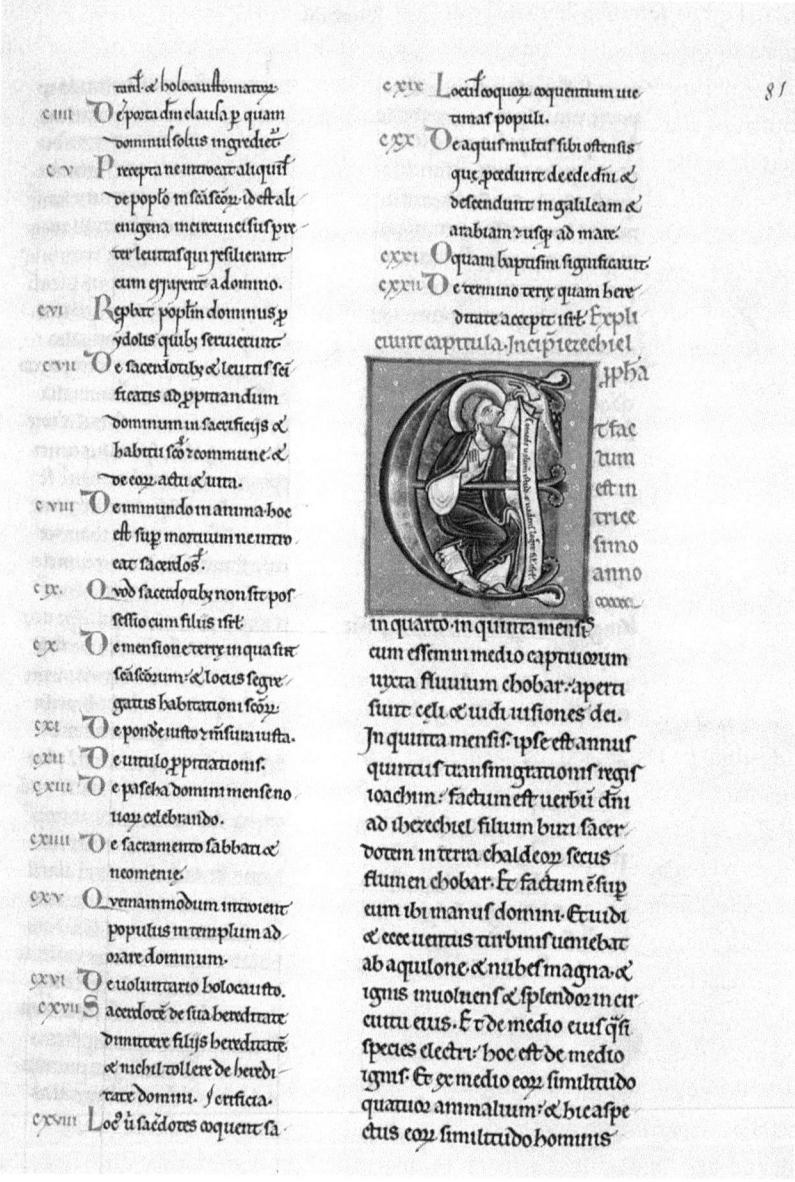

Figure 9 Banderole from Paris, BnF ms. Latin 16744, 12th-century Bible, f. 81r

look in wonder at the "scientific" history practices in the academy, and feel at home in these embodied performances of monasticism, is an important data point.

Other participants felt that the performances taught something about iterability in monastic life. One medievalist art history Ph.D. student attended the performance event twice: first in November, and again in February.[30] In February, she noted that in November she hadn't really been "feeling it" – it was the end of the semester, and she was tired. She'd left slightly bored in November and was bummed when a class of hers was attending the event in February. But in February, at the beginning of the semester, she came to the event with a renewed and restful mind and newly felt that it was interesting. She likened her experience to making a particular dish from a recipe – while one goes through the same motions, the taste is never the same. Sometimes you use a different oven; sometimes you get a particularly flavorful crop of spinach; sometimes you forget the salt; sometimes you're very hungry when you eat the finished product – there is no objectivity to witnessing, it is different every time. This, she claimed, must also be the problem with the archive – sometimes you're tired and you miss something; sometimes you want to get a drink with your friends after, and all of that desire stilts your 'objectivity.' The experience of repeat performances at The Met Cloisters made her realize this and will transform her work going forward.

Another participant, a professional dance educator and dance-maker from NYU, had observations to make about how the event helped her understand historical temporality differently. Her own understanding of her lineage as an artist came from her personal archive of photos and videos of her work, in a similar way to her own family history, which began in earnest in her mind only when there were physical documents from their lives (stories, photos, objects, or videos). She found it "thrilling," through the performance-lecture, to witness how the past could be accessed "back so much further" through work that aims "to un-sediment the presence of the body." In a way, to her, this engagement of the body felt like "culturally-responsive pedagogy" to the premodern world. She also was reminded of her pandemic experience, and how throughout the COVID-19 lockdown we had all gained "such wisdom" on "how to be in space and time" – wisdom more akin to monastic life than modern life, it seemed to her.

These comments, a small selection from the many I received in the 30-minute post-performance discussions I moderated after the five performance-lectures, reminded me of a comment made by the ninth-century monk and theologian Hrabanus Maurus, who claimed that his famous *carmina figurata, In honorem crucis,* were tools made not to provide his readers with *one* answer to

---

[30] A Brooklyn College student wrote about this February event in the *Brooklyn College Vanguard*, the student newspaper: https://vanguard.blog.brooklyn.edu/2024/02/08/experiencing-medieval-monasticism-at-the-cloisters/.

a devotional problem, but *many routes* to enabling their own active devotional investigations:

> In this work I am the translator or interpreter in some fashion, not of another language, but of another kind of speech, in order that I might explain the truth of the same sense. For this reason, I ask the reader not to receive our work disdainfully, and ... may he be a participant in eternal rejoicing with us (Kumler, 2023, p. 103).

"May [the reader] be a participant" in the activity of knowledge-making is Hrabanus' hope, declared as a preface to his work. In a similar way, these performance-lectures allowed for audiences to make historical and epistemological discoveries on their own and with their own bodies, allowing for a more significant impact (and a more internalized, embodied set of discoveries) than a "normal," disembodied, wholly analytical academic talk.

5.2.2 Museums Are Biased Spaces, and Limit Our Abilities to Perceive the Past as Historians

The Met Cloisters was an ideal setting for these performances investigating medieval monasticism – after all, it is a uniquely atmospheric medieval museum, one of the only ones in North America, and at its core features a 12th-century chapel, chapter house, and cloister, roughly ordered in alignment with the prescribed arrangement of these spaces in the Middle Ages according to the plan of St. Gall (Husband, 2013). The Met Cloisters does not typically house medieval objects behind glass cases or hang them on white-washed walls; instead, it aims to present them *in situ*, roughly displayed as they were in their medieval context. The Met Cloisters galleries, then, are fundamentally experiential, "recreating a virtual world into which their visitor enters," one imitating the historical world so much that it seems "anterior, if subsequent, to the representation" (Kirshenblatt-Gimblett, 1998, pp. 3–4).

And yet, The Met Cloisters is by no means immune to the "civilizing rituals inside public art museums" (Duncan, 1995). The art is carefully guarded by at least one museum guard in each gallery; the objects are all labeled, cleaned, unused, and roped off; and the art remains first and foremost presented for pure, artificially-siloed "aesthetic inspiration," "drain[ed of] ... natural and supernatural agencies and enchantments" (Promey, 2017, p. xx). Moreover, as a secular institution in North America in a city as religiously diverse as New York, the museum evinces "an ongoing discomfort with anything more than the most superficial explanations about religious practices and rituals, especially those associated with Christianity" (Freudenheim, 2017, p. 181). While it seems to promise an experience of the medieval world akin to that of the seventeenth century delivered at Plimoth Plantation, where visitors are comfortable exploring and improvising with actors playing seventeenth-century characters, The Met Cloisters, despite its layout, feels more high-art proper, pent up and elite, expecting hushed tones and educated mumbles rather than the performances these now-taxidermized objects likely witnessed at their points of origin one thousand years ago. At The Met Cloisters, rational, intellectual knowledge is meant to disarm the impulse toward phenomenological knowledge that the layout inspires and the emotionality that the space hints at. Despite its atmospheric intentions, The Met Cloisters is more art museum than medieval space (O'Doherty, 1976).

The performance-lectures, however, activated the medieval-ness of the space. Several participants had been to the space before, and the non-medievalists especially had never seen it as anything but a stuffy and impenetrable museum. Through the performance-lecture, however, participants explained that the museum-ness of the space melted away, and the exploration felt more "ascetic than aesthetic," with participants learning to more viscerally and experientially understand "how difficult it was for medieval monks to tune out the world around them and tune into the divine." The performance-lectures disabled the uptightness of museum-going and instead "enabled an immense freedom." One participant felt "a deluge of resonance"; for another, "a spiritual synapse opened." A professor of early modern history expressed that it allowed him to "imagine an experiential world that lies beyond my intellectual grasp." A medievalist graduate student explained that performing helped her

> tap into the humanity of the people I study. It's the difference between saying something and actually doing it. When we're temporally and culturally so far from those people (and when so many of our texts from the period are anonymous) objectifying them is easier than one might want to admit. The exercises at the event helped me feel (embody?) what it means to think of medieval people as *subjects*.

5.2.3 The Communal Perception of History Is Democratizing and Generative

History is more often than not written by solo individuals. We sit next to each other in the library or the archive, but mostly this is parallel play – rarely do we collaborate, and when we do, it is usually in pairs, not in lab-sized groups.[31] For a long time, medievalists have tried to understand the experience of the individual and the 'invention of the self' in medieval monasticism (Melville, 2002).

---

[31] The exception to this is in European contexts, where many collaborative team projects are funded.

Part of the reason why this has been such a fascinating topic is that it is hard for us modern historians to imagine an interiority that was not experienced alone, but was instead experienced as a group in the Middle Ages (Bynum, 1980; Boynton, 2007). But medieval monasticism was essentially and fundamentally an experience of community; it was through the community that the individual grew, not only because of the policing and surveillance endemic to community, but also because the container the community provided for spiritual growth was a kind of proof that love – *caritas* – was real. They would eat, work, and pray together for much of the day. They would sleep together in a communal dorm. The community would see the bad and the good in any individual monk – there was no escape from such vulnerability – and was instructed to radically accept the bad and the good, a kind of proof of Christian love (Sonntag, 2011). The individual subject was not formed without the experience of the collective, and the individual's thought and experience were not developed in anchoritic isolation.

How contrary to the modern historian's experience, then, was the knowledge production of the monastery? Historians today often work alone; we research alone; we edit alone; we give feedback alone. Often, lecturing at the head of the classroom, we teach alone. When we give papers, we often are isolated at the head of the conference room; even 'roundtables' are, in the hands of academics, rarely real discussions and exchanges. Since we are so isolated in our making of history, how well-honed could our perception of communal historical people possibly be?

The most remarkable part of the performance-lectures at The Met Cloisters was that they were embodied and *everyone* was participating. No one could be passive. No one could avoid at least *attempting* physical, vocal, gustatory, and sonic activation. The performance-lectures at The Met Cloisters did "discover" some concrete things about the medieval monastic past. We now better understand how to analyze the monastic sign language for "to tell a lie." We now better understand just how much our secular world has biased our perception of medieval Christianity. But I think the most important thing that these lectures did – more than discovering truths about the monastic past – was that they reoriented a piece of the scholar-community that created that past. In my view, premodern monks have more in common with collaborative post-modern performance artists than with the historians who study them today.[32] There was no constructing knowledge in a disembodied way alone in the medieval monastery

---

[32] See my forthcoming piece, "You Had to Be There: Approaching Medieval Monastic Religious Experience Through a Twentieth-Century Lens," in *Fragments of Experience: Approaching "Lived Religion" from Late Antiquity to the Central Middle Ages*, Lauren Mancia and Brian Sowers, editors (volume currently under review with Bloomsbury).

(even original written texts were knowledge created in community). There were no passive monks in eleventh- and twelfth-century medieval monasteries. There was no performative frame in medieval monastic ritual – the proscenium of Western theater is a modern invention. Instead, monks were equal participant-observers in a horizontal, communal medieval liturgy that served to both memorialize biblical events and also enact them in real time. Monks understood their rituals BOTH intellectually – connected to moralizing, exegetical readings of the Bible – and phenomenologically, happening to them experientially and emotionally in the present moment, and in a liturgical cycle for all eternity. Monastic performances were not saints' stories played in a theater to a silent, inert audience, or a sermon told to a bunch of dozing monks. Participatory understanding was fundamental to the way that monks understood their religion experientially, and in medieval monastic performances, monks regularly, aggressively shocked themselves into engagement, so that they could intellectually, mnemonically, and viscerally comprehend their devotional activities. When historians shock themselves into practice, when they *DO* in public, next to each other, what do they learn about themselves and, therefore, their subjects of study?

What I think is so valuable about the enacted performance of monastic behavior, rather than the observation of that behavior as represented in archival sources and texts, or even the imagination of that behavior in one's mind, is that it opens a performative dimension[33] allowing historians to become perforated by the actions of medieval monks. By witnessing objects and subjects of the past in an embodied way, by trying to write with monks and not just about them, by making and doing in order to know, what historical discoveries can we unearth? We cannot recreate the full contexts that led medieval monks into their vocation, that would let us experience language, or emotion, or space, or community in a way parallel to how medieval monks did 1,000 years ago, of course. But just as our bodies are not products of medieval monastic culture, and therefore inadequate to the task of recreating the Middle Ages, merely reading and writing about monasticism in a disembodied way prevents historians from comprehending pieces of medieval culture that reperformance might awaken.

Tavia Nyong'O talks about creative anachronism as particularly repellent to historians because we deeply believe in the virtues of our professionalism and believe that amateurs – like historical reenactors – don't "get history right." But Nyong'O provocatively asks: *why don't we worry about the ethics of the chance that our professionalism gets it wrong?* (Nyong'O, 2009, p. 136). Isn't the risk of romanticization, embarrassment, and bodily presence involved in this

---

[33] I am indebted to Eleonora Fabião for this phrase.

performance exercise worth it if it means we won't neglect the history of affective experience? Isn't the "unscientific" approach of these performances worth the risk if they more fully reveal our subjects? Today, the scholarship of "doubting, of unease, of trouble, [and] of alarm" seems truer than earnest "scholarship with a noble aim" (Brook, 1995, p. 45). If a scholarly audience drops all its defenses and allows itself to be perforated and taken in by performance, how might our field – and our understanding of historical experience – transform?

5.3 We Can Take These Performances to the Next Level

This Element has been an outline of a methodology that I intend as a provocation for historians – it is not a call for us to abandon our archival research practices, but a wakeup call for us to begin to see how our disembodiment and our lack of self-knowledge inhibit our historical work. The performance-lectures I tried over the course of a year are pretty timid exercises relative to what this methodology could potentially be in its fullest form. They just scratched the surface of turning the scholarly ego off. Participants still looked at the museum labels. They could perform at only 50 percent, hiding behind the excuse of being in a public space with other nonparticipating museum visitors. Many participants clamored for the exercise to be longer than forty-five minutes in future iterations, to begin at the entrance to Fort Tryon Park, ten minutes before they entered the museum; others wanted instructions that would begin when they woke up that morning – a diet, a clothing ritual, a soundtrack. They felt their bodies needed more time to calibrate and settle into the activities before they could discover anything truly, deeply useful. They were "in synch but also out of synch." The experience of surrender had only just started by the end of the exercise, and they longed for a more durational experience so that they could pair the frustration and failure they felt for much of the forty-five minutes with some other information about what would happen over the course of a day (or a lifetime) of monastic practice. We would need to weave a whole bunch of performances like this together to achieve any kind of real knowledge about the past. But what *was* achieved after forty-five minutes was an instigation to more original, or to different, historical ways of thinking on the part of all of the scholars who participated. In a way, that's what mattered the most: that embodiment broke our old thought patterns and opened up new ways of considering the past.

For me, the experience of surrender was hard to achieve because, as the leader, I was preoccupied with curating the experience – keeping an eye on the museum guards, the other museum visitors, and the participants themselves removed me from the ritual in The Met Cloisters. But I had my own opportunity to surrender to *doing* that I can share, adjacent to these performance-lectures. In December 2023, after studying medieval monasticism for twenty years, I spent my first week in a monastery (that none of my professors had ever suggested I do this is another data point for the disembodied tendencies of historians). I spent my first day at the monastery totally in my head, taking notes all the time. This lasted until the first Eucharist I attended, about twenty hours after I'd arrived. When I had sat down for the mass, I was not very excited: as a scholar, I had always found the mass less interesting than the monastic office because it felt less idiosyncratic, less textually surprising. So I sat in my seat ready to be bored. All of a sudden, after having experienced hours of the monophonic chant of the office, the monks broke into polyphony, the first polyphony I had heard in their church during my trip. I immediately burst into tears – the shock of the beauty and contrast of the polyphonic soundscape was so arresting. I had *intellectually* known that polyphony would be reserved for the mass, the transcendence of the Eucharistic ritual encapsulated thereby. But I had never *experienced* the ineffable quality of that transcendent song, nor had I ever experienced the emotional contrast between the divine office sung in unison for much of the day, and the divergent moment of resplendent, discordant, harmonious mass. The whole space of the church changed – somehow the air was different, the light was different, the community was different. An aura of awe infused the room and remained among us for the entirety of the mass period (Moxey, 2013, p. 124; Meyer, 2015). I was disarmed and vulnerable for the remainder of that first mass (And after this experience, I edited my performance-lecture scripts to add a moment of song to our score.)

When it came time for the Eucharist to be given to the community, I was again totally surprised. While I had witnessed the celebration of the Eucharist many times before, I had only seen it in churches where priests ministered to lay people. In those environments, a hierarchy always emerged, whether it was intended or not: the celebrant, who was purveying the Eucharist in his distinctive vestments, had a kind of exclusive, all-knowing quality, and the lay people, lining up to receive with their hands outstretched, appeared as beggars, a level below the celebrant. However, this Eucharist, my first celebrated among monks, was radically horizontal: the monks, all wearing identical robes, appeared to be celebrating a ritual among equals in the community. Each day I was there, a different monk was the appointed celebrant, which only added to the humble and communal flavor of the ritual – one day, monk X played the celebrant and monk Y played the supplicant; and the next day, monk Y played the celebrant and monk X played the supplicant. By the end of my stay, the Eucharist was my favorite event of the day – I couldn't wait for that burst of polyphonic sound to elevate the otherwise calm but monotonous soundscape of the monastery. And I couldn't wait to watch the monastic community members alternately minister and submit to each other during their ingestion of the body and blood of Jesus, in a state of radical horizontality. Even though I had dedicated an entire chapter to the theology and mysticism of the Eucharist in monasteries in my first book (Mancia, 2019, Chapter Four), I finally, viscerally understood what all the fuss was about the Eucharist in the monastery, and why this ritual was so awe-inspiring to its eleventh-century monastic witnesses.

My experience at the mass was the most profound one that I had during my monastic stay. But that week at the monastery, there were other, more subtle, embodied transformations of my understanding of monastic life, too. After two days in the monastery, I viscerally understood things about temporality in the medieval monastery that I had not understood, no matter how many books on the monastic liturgy I read. After three days, I viscerally understood that one could not focus on anything for more than two hours before one was called back into the church to sing the office. After five days, I viscerally understood that the time on my watch didn't mean anything, but the church's bells were what determined my body's rhythms. I learned what time to go to bed so I could wake early in the morning and (literally) have a voice with which to sing before eating or drinking anything. Was there something more ethical about experimenting with my own body to investigate medieval monasticism, rather than simply proclaiming historical truths from the safety of my office armchair? Perhaps. But the real point is that I learned things after *days* – a fraction of the time that the monks themselves practice these activities – but much longer than the 45 minutes I provided the performance-lecture participants.[34] How much had I missed as a historian of monasticism, having just lived in my intellect for so long? My Ph.D. training had disabused me of many horrible assumptions that I had about the medieval period – but that intellectual training alone had only gotten me so far. *Doing* monasticism for a week had gotten me so much more data, such that I felt I was so much closer to understanding the distant land of the medieval past than I had been after twenty years of training as a medievalist. Of course, my experience in a contemporary monastery in the United States in 2024 was not *precise* information about the *real* medieval monastic world. But my time in the monastery still was a reorientation that would allow me to ask historical questions differently, a liberation from both modern expectations and the textual constraints I hadn't realized I was imposing upon myself. I felt as if my imagination had opened, and I had knocked down some wall that I had previously written off as permanently impenetrable.

---

[34] I am currently working on a scholarly article about these experiences in the monastery.

Scholars are lucky enough to have venues in which to regularly experiment together with performance. Conferences last for days – weekends, sometimes even weeks – and are often in person. Summer and intercession breaks are often months long. What would happen if we used conferences for performance experiments, as well as more traditional academic papers? The International Congress on Medieval Studies at Western Michigan University in Kalamazoo (that happens every May) regularly has medieval music performances or mead-making demonstrations; the International Medieval Congress at the University of Leeds (which happens every July) regularly has falconry demonstrations or even jousts. The American Historical Association conference (that happens every January) regularly has walking tours. But these are lectures or entertainments – scholars do not *embody* and *perform research by doing*; they watch as passive audience members. What if, in the middle of Western Michigan's campus, I walled myself into a structure as an anchorite and performed medieval anchoritism for four days?[35] What if a group of scholars went on pilgrimage to Canterbury from Leeds, on foot, during the July conference? What if I gave my conference paper in the style of a medieval university classroom *lectio* during the January AHA conference? Such performances could happen outside of conferences, too. What if I wrote a scholarly monograph in the style of a medieval scholastic treatise (like Even-Ezra, 2021)? What if I gathered medievalists who work on monasticism in NYC to sing the monastic office together every morning in the summertime before we all started our days? Historians of drama and music know what they must *do* in order to understand; historians of art know that they must visit the monuments they study, not just rely on images; why don't we historians learn this lesson? I posit that experimentation with the reperformance of medieval actions will allow us to better understand medieval history through our own embodied inquiry. Each experiment with reperformance would necessarily be incomplete – each would end with only a partial answer to a historical question, leaving participants asking more questions than satisfied with solutions. But the effect could be cumulative over a scholar's life.

Still, though performance can blunt cynicism in historians and might enkindle in us a *longing* to better understand, it can never deliver complete understanding. But such incompleteness is a very historically accurate feeling for the Middle Ages (Mancia, 2023). Moreover, this kind of partial answer, the inchoate hint at an idea that results from performance, is a more realistic representation of historical experience than a list of definite historical facts would be. If the experience of most historical people was that of *making*, of becoming, and

---

[35] I am currently planning on staging such a reperformance in 2026 and 2027.

incompleteness, then such reperformances, seemingly deficient, might actually be better encapsulations of lived historical experience as incomplete and in process, confounding, to be sure, but also active and ever-evolving, in a constant state of *in medias res*. Reperforming history yields information essential to understanding history, and so it is essential for historians to practice performance. This is precisely because the knowledge acquired through performance is different from typical historical knowledge: ultimately, it's a kind of knowledge that you can't entirely explain with words, but are sure in your body that you have acquired.

References

Primary Sources

Aelred of Rievaulx. (1971). *Treatises and Pastoral Prayer.* Kalamazoo, MI: Cistercian.

Anselm of Canterbury. (1975). *The Prayers and Meditations of Saint Anselm of Canterbury*, trans. Benedicta Ward. New York: Penguin.

Bernard of Clairvaux. (1987). *Selected Works*, trans. G. R. Evans. Mahwah, NJ: Paulist Press.

Constable, Giles, ed. (2008). *Three Treatises from Bec on the Nature of Monastic Life.* Toronto: University of Toronto Press.

Guigo II. (1981). *Ladder of Monks and Twelve Meditations.* Collegeville, MI: Liturgical Press.

John of Fécamp. (1946). *Un maitre de la vie spirituelle de Xie siecle*, ed. Jean Leclercq /Jean-Paul Bonnes. Paris: J. Vrin.

Peter of Celle. (1987). *Selected Works*. Kalamazoo, MI: Cistercian.

William of St. Thierry. (1970). *On Contemplating: "On Contemplating God: Prayer, Meditations"* trans. Penelope Lawson. Kalamazoo, MI: Cistercian.

Secondary Sources

Adler, Gillian. (2022). *Chaucer and the Ethics of Time.* Cardiff: University of Wales Press.

Agamben, Giorgio. (2007). *Infancy and History: On the Destruction of Experience*, trans. Liz Heron. New York: Verso Books.

Ahmed, Sara. (2006). *Queer Phenomenology: Orientations, Objects, Others.* Durham, NC: Duke University Press.

Althoff, Gerd. (2020). *Rules and Rituals in Medieval Power Games.* Turnhout: Brill.

Ankersmit, Frank. (2005). *Sublime Historical Experience.* Stanford, CA: Stanford University Press.

Asad, Talal. (1987). On Ritual and Discipline in Medieval Christian Monasticism. *Economy and Society*, 16 (2), pp. 159–203

Asad, Talal. (1993). *Genealogies of Religion: Discipline and Reasons of Power in Christianity and Islam.* Baltimore, MD: Johns Hopkins University Press.

Asad, Talal. (1997). Remarks on the Anthropology of the Body. In *Religion and the Body*, Sarah Coakley, ed. New York: Cambridge University Press, pp. 42–53.

Auslander, Mark. (2013). Touching the Past: Materializing Time in Traumatic "Living History" Reenactments. *Sign and Society*, 1 (1), pp. 161–183.

Austin, J. L. (1975). *How to Do Things with Words*. New York: Oxford University Press.

Bahktin, Mikhail. (2021). Rabelais and His World. In *The Applied Theater Reader*. Second Ed., Tim Prentki and Nicola Abraham, eds. New York: Routledge, pp. 22–28.

Basso, Keith H. (1996). *Wisdom Sits in Places: Landscape and Language among the Western Apache*. Santa Fe, NM: University of New Mexico Press.

Baxandall, Michael. (1988). *Painting and Experience in Fifteenth-Century Italy*. New York: Oxford University Press.

Beckwith, Sarah. (2001). *Signifying God: Social Relation and Symbolic Act in the York Corpus Christi Plays*. Chicago, IL: University of Chicago Press.

Bentacourt, Roland. (2016). Imagined Encounters: Historiographies for a New World. *Postmedieval*, 7 (1), pp. 3–9.

Berlant, Lauren. (2008). *The Female Complaint: The Unfinished Business of Sentimentality in American Culture*. Durham, NC: Duke University Press.

Biddick, Kathleen. (1998). *The Shock of Medievalism*. Durham, NC: Duke University Press.

Bissell, Bill and Linda Caruso Haviland, eds. (2018). Introduction. In *The Sentient Archive: Bodies, Performance, Memory*. Middletown, CT: Wesleyan University, pp. 1–17.

Blanc, Aurélie. (2024). *Female Performance and Spectatorship in a Medieval Nunnery: The* Elevatio *and* Visitatio Sepulchri *of Barking Abbey in Practice*. Leeds: ARC Humanities Press.

Bloch, Maurice. (1989). *Ritual, History, Power: Selected Papers in Anthropology*. New York: Routledge.

Boddice, Rob and Mark Smith. (2020). *Emotion, Sense, Experience*. Cambridge Elements: Histories of Emotions and the Senses. New York: Cambridge University Press.

Bordo, Susan R. (1987). *The Flight to Objectivity: Essays on Cartesianism and Culture*. Albany: State University of New York Press.

Boynton, Susan. (2007). Prayer as Liturgical Performance in Eleventh- and Twelfth-Century Monastic Psalters. *Speculum*, 82 (4), pp. 895–931.

Brook, Peter. (1995). *The Empty Space: A Book about the Theater: Deadly, Holy, Rough, Immediate*. New York: Scribner.

Bruce, Scott. (2007). *Silence and Sign Langauge in Medieval Monasticism: The Cluniac Tradition, c. 900–1200*. New York: Cambridge University Press.

Bryan-Wilson, Julia. (2018). *Sharon Hayes (Phaidon Contemporary Artists Series)*. New York: Phaidon.

Buchak, Laura. (2014). Belief, Credence, and Norms. *Philosophical Studies*, 169 (2), pp. 285–311.

Buck-Morss, Susan. (2021). *Year One: A Philosophical Recounting*. Cambridge, MA: Massachusetts Institute for Technology Press.

Burke, Peter. (2005). Performing History: The Importance of Occasions. *Rethinking History*, 9 (1), pp. 35–52.

Burrus, Virginia. (2018). *Ancient Christian Ecopoetics: Cosmologies, Saints, Things*. Philadelphia: University of Pennsylvania Press.

Bynum, Caroline Walker. (1980). Did the Twelfth Century Discover the Individual? *The Journal of Ecclesiastical History*, 31 (1), pp. 1–17.

Bynum, Caroline Walker. (2017). *The Resurrection of the Body in Western Christianity, 200–1336*. New York: Columbia University Press.

Caldwell, Mary Channen. (2022). *Devotional Refrains in Medieval Latin Song*. Cambridge: Cambridge University Press.

Callaghan, David. (2013). Ritual Performance and Spirituality in the Work of the Living Theatre, Past and Present. *Theatre Symposium*, 21, pp. 36–53.

Carlson, Marvin. (2016). *Shattering Hamlet's Mirror: Theatre and Reality*. Ann Arbor, MI: University of Michigan Press.

Carruthers, Mary. (1998). *The Book of Memory*. New York: Cambridge University Press.

Carruthers, Mary. (2010). The Concept of "Ductus," or, Journeying through a Work of Art. In *Rhetoric beyond Words: Delight and Persuasion in the Arts*, Mary Carruthers, ed. New York: Cambridge University Press, pp. 190–214.

Carruthers, Mary J. (1990). *The Book of Memory: A Study of Memory in Medieval Culture*. New York: Cambridge University Press.

Chaganti, Seeta. (2023). Dance, Institution, Abolition. *Postmedieval*, 14 (2), pp. 267–289.

Chakrabarty, Dipesh. (2002). *Habitations of Modernity: Essays in the Wake of Subaltern Studies*. Chicago, IL: University of Chicago Press.

Chambers, Claire Maria, Simon du Toit, and Joshua Edelman, eds. (2013). Introduction. In *Performing Religion in Public*. New York: Palgrave, pp. 1–21.

Chazelle, Celia. (2007). *The Crucified God in the Carolingian Ear: Theology and Art of Christ's Passion*. New York: Cambridge University Press.

Chin, Catherine Michael. (2023) Idiot Late Antiquity: History, Scale, and Play. In *Scale and the Study of Late Antiquity*, Kevin Uhalde and Kristina Sessa, eds. Bari: Edipuglia, pp. 1–15.

Chin, Catherine Michael. (2024). *Life: The Natural History of an Early Christian Universe*. Berkeley: University of California Press.

Collingwood, R. G. (1972). *The Idea of History*. New York: Oxford University Press.

Constable, Giles. (1990). A Living Past: The Historical Environment of the Middle Ages. *Harvard Library Bulletin*, 1 (3), pp. 49–70.

Conquergood, Dwight. (2013). *Cultural Struggles: Performance, Ethnography, Praxis*. Ann Arbor, MI: University of Michigan.

Davis, Kathleen. (2017). *Periodization and Sovreignty: How Ideas of Feudalism and Secularization Govern the Politcs of Time*. Philadelphia: University of Pennsylvania Press.

Davis, Natalie Zemon. (1990). *Fiction in the Archives: Pardon Tales and Their Tellers in Sixteenth-Century France*. Palo Alto, CA: Stanford University Press.

de Certeau, Michel. (1981). Une practique sociale de la différance: croire. In *Faire Croire: Modalités de la diffusion et la reception des messages religieux du XIIe au XVe siècle: Actes de table ronde de Rome (22–23 juin 1979)*, André Vauchez, ed. Paris: École française de Rome, pp. 363–383.

Deleuze, Gilles. (1995). *Difference and Repetition*, ed. Paul Patton. New York: Columbia University Press.

Derrida, Jacques. (1998). *Archive Fever: A Freudian Impression*. Chicago, IL: University of Chicago Press.

Dilthy, Wilhelm. (2002). *The Formation of the Historical World in the Human Sciences*. Princeton, NJ: Princeton University Press.

Dinshaw, Carolyn. (2012). *How Soon Is Now? Medieval Texts, Amateur Readers, and the Queerness of Time*. Durham, NC: Duke University Press.

Dox, Donnalee. (2004). *The Idea of the Theatre in Latin Christian Thought: Augustine to the Fourteenth Century*. Ann Arbor, MI: University of Michigan Press.

Dox, Donnalee. (2016). *Reckoning with the Spirit in the Paradigm of Performance*. Ann Arbor, MI: University of Michigan Press.

Dray, William. (1999). *History as Re Enactment: R.G. Collingwood's Idea of History*. New York: Oxford University Press.

Dror, Otniel E. (2020). Historians in the Emotion Laboratory. *Emotions Review*, 12 (3), pp. 191–192.

Duncan, Carol. (1995). *Civilizing Rituals: Inside Public Art Museums*. New York: Routledge.

Dutton, Elisabeth. (2019). A Manifesto for Performace Research. In *The Methuen Drama Handbook of Theatre History and Historiography*, Clare Cochrane and Joanna Robinson, eds. London: Bloomsbury, pp. 249–261.

Eire, Carlos M. N. (2023). *They Flew: A History of the Impossible*. New Haven, CT: Yale University Press.

Enders, Jody. (1992). *Rhetoric and the Origin of Medieval Drama*. Ithaca, NY: Cornell University Press.

Even-Ezra, Ayelet. (2021). *Lines of Thought: Branching Diagrams and the Medieval Mind*. Chicago, IL: University of Chicago Press.

Fabião, Eleonora. (2006). *Precarious, Precarious, Precarious Performative Historiography and the Energetics of the Paradox: Arthur Bispo do Rosario's and Lygia Clark's Works in Rio de Janeiro*. Ph.D Dissertation, New York University, Department of Performance Studies.

Farjoun, Amir. (2024). *Epistemic Theatres: The Dramaturgy of Knowledge in Twenty-First Century Theatre*. Ph.D Dissertation, CUNY Graduate Center.

Farrugia, Peter. (2024). *"Tout est possible!"* Using Historical Re-enactment in a University Classroom. *The History Teacher*, 57 (4), pp. 441–465.

Fassler, Margot. (2010). *The Virgin of Chartres: Making History through Liturgy*. New Haven, CT: Yale University Press.

Feiss, Hugh. (2024). *Meditation and Prayer in the Eleventh- and Twelfth-Century Monastery: Struggling towards God* (review). *American Benedictine Review*, 75 (1), pp. 103–104.

Ferrer, Jorge N. and Jacob H. Sherman, eds. (2009). *The Participatory Turn: Spirituality, Mysticism, Religious Studies*. Albany: State University of New York Press.

Foucault, Michel. (1995). *Discipline and Punish*. New York: Vintage.

Frank, Rike. (2013). When Form Starts Talking: Lecture-Performances. *Konstfack* 33. www.konstfack.se/PageFiles/17986/Afterall_When%20Form%20Starts%20Talking_%20On%20Lecture-Performances.pdf.

Freire, Paulo. (2000). *Pedagogy of the Oppressed*. New York: Bloomsbury.

Freudenheim, Tom. (2017). Museums and Religion: Uneasy Companions. In *Religion in Museums: Global and Multidisciplinary Perspectives*, Gretchen Buggeln, Crispin Paine, S. Brent Plate, eds. New York: Bloomsbury, pp. 181–189.

Fricke, Beate and Aden Kumler, eds. (2022). *Destroyed, Disappeared, Lost, Never Were*. University Park, PA: Penn State University Press.

Fulton, Rachel. (1996). Mimetic Devotion, Marian Exegesis, and the Historical Sense of the Song of Songs. *Viator*, 27, pp. 85–116.

Fulton Brown, Rachel. (2017). *Mary and the Art of Prayer: The Hours of the Virgin in Medieval Christian Life and Thought*. New York: Columbia University Press.

Gadamer, Hans-Georg. (1997). *Truth and Method*, trans. Joel Weinshiemer. New York: Continuum.

Garbes, Angela. (2022). *Essential Labor: Mothering as Social Change.* New York: Harper Collins.

Gasparini, Valentino, Maik Patzelt, Rubina Raja, et al., eds. (2020). *Lived Religion in the Ancient Mediterranean World: Approaching Religious Transformations from Archaeology, History, and Classics.* Berlin: DeGruter.

Gertsman, Elina. (2015). *Worlds Within: Opening the Medieval Shrine Madonna.* University Park, PA: Penn State University Press.

Gharavi, Lance. (2013). About[/]Doing: Religion and Theater in the Academy. In *Religion, Theater, and Performance*, Lance Gharavi, ed. New York: Routledge, pp. 210–219.

Giannachi, Gabriella and Nick Kaye. (2011). *Performing Presence: Between the Live and the Simulated.* Manchester: Manchester University Press.

Goffman, Erving. (1959). *The Presentation of Self in Everyday Life.* New York: Doubleday.

Gordon, Avery F. (2008). *Ghostly Matters: Haunting and the Sociological Imagination.* Minneapolis: University of Minnesota Press.

Hahn, Cynthia. (2017). The Graphic Cross as Salvific Mark and Organizing Principle: Making, Marking, Shaping. In *Graphic Devices and the Early Decorated Book*, Michelle Brown, Ildar H. Garipzanov, and Benjamin C. Tilghman, eds. Martlesham: Boydell and Brewer, pp. 100–125.

Hammann, Byron Ellsworth. (2016). How to Chronologize with a Hammer, or, the Myth of Homogeneous, Empty Time. *HAU: Journal of Ethnographic Theory*, 6 (1), pp. 261–292.

Hardison, O. B. (1965). *Christian Rite and Christian Drama in the Middle Ages: Essays in the Origin and Early History of Modern Drama.* Baltimore, MD: Johns Hopkins University Press.

Hartman, Saidiya. (1997). *Scenes of Subjection: Terror, Slavery, and Self-Making in Nineteenth-Century America.* New York: Oxford University Press.

Hartman, Saidiya. (2008). Venus in Two Acts. *Small Axe*, 12 (2), pp. 1–14.

Heller, Nathan. (2024). The Battle for Attention. *The New Yorker*, April 29, 2024. https://www.newyorker.com/magazine/2024/05/06/the-battle-for-attention.

Hen, Yitzak and Matthew Innes, eds. (2000). *The Uses of the Past in the Early Middle Ages.* New York: Cambridge University Press.

Huizinga, Johan. (1954). *The Waning of the Middle Ages: A Study of the Forms of Life, Thought, and Art in France and the Netherlands in the 14th and 15th centuries.* New York: Anchor Press.

Hunt, Lynn. (2009). The Experience of Revolution. *French Historical Studies*, 32 (4), pp. 671–678.

Husband, Timothy B. (2013). *Creating the Cloisters*. New York: Metropolitan Museum of Art.

Husemann, Pirkko. (2004). The Absent Presence of Artistic Working Processes. The Lecture as Format of Performance. Frankfurt. www.unfriendly-takeover.de/downloads/f14_husemann_engl.pdf.

Ingold, Tim. (2013). *Making: Anthropology, Archaeology, Art, and Architecture*. New York: Routledge.

Irvine, Richard D. G. (2010). The Experience of Ethnographic Fieldwork in an English Benedictine Monastery: Or, Not Playing at Being a Monk. *Fieldwork in Religion*, 5 (2), pp. 221–235.

Jackson, Ken and Arthur F. Marotti. (2004). The Turn to Religion in Early Modern English Studies. *Criticism*, 46 (1), pp.167–190.

Jackson, Reginald. (2021). *A Proximate Remove: Queering Intimacy and Loss in* The Tale of Genji. Berkeley: University of California Press.

Jakobsen, Janet R. and Ann Pellegrini. (2008). *Secularisms*. Durham, NC: Duke University Press.

James, William. (1971). *Essays in Radical Empiricism and a Pluralistic Universe*. New York: Dutton.

James, William. (2009). *The Varieties of Religious Experience*. New York: Random House.

Jarausch, Konrad. (1989). Towards a History of Experience: Postmodern Predicaments in Theory and Interdisciplinarity. *Central European History*, 22 (¾), pp. 427–443.

Jay, Martin. (2005). *Songs of Experience: Modern American and European Variations on a Universal Theme*. Berkeley: University of California Press.

Jucan, Ioana B., Jussi Parikka, and Rebecca Schneider. (2018). *Remain*. Lüneburg: Meson Press.

Jung, Jacqueline E. (2020). *Eloquent Bodies: Movement, Expression, and the Human Figure in Gothic Sculpture*. New Haven, CT: Yale University Press.

Katajala-Peltomaa, Sari and Raisa Maria Toivo, eds. (2022). *Histories of Experience in the World of Lived Religion*. New York: Palgrave.

Kemp, Amanda. (1998). This Black Body in Question. In *The Ends of Performance*, Peggy Phalen and Jill Lane, eds. New York: New York University Press, pp. 116–131.

Kerr, Julie. (2009). *Life in the Medieval Cloister*. New York: Continuum Press.

Kirshenblatt-Gimblett, Barbara. (1998). *Destination Culture: Tourism, Museums, Heritage*. Berkeley: University of California Press.

Kitzinger, Beatrice. (2019). *The Cross, the Gospels, and the Work of Art in the Carolingian Age*. New York: Cambridge University Press.

Kleinberg, Ethan, Joan Wallach Scott, and Gary Wilder. (2020). Theses on Theory and History, with Comments. *History of the Present*, 10 (1), pp. 157–165.

Kumler, Aden. (2023). All Form Is a Process of Notation: Hrabanus Maurus' "Exemplativist" Art. In *L'art medieval est-il contemporain?* Charlotte Denoël, Larisa Dryansky, Isabelle Marchesin, and Erik Verhagen, eds. Turnhout: Brepols, pp. 91–112.

Logan, Dana W. (2022). *Awkward Rituals: Sensations of Governance in Protestant America*. Chicago, IL: University of Chicago Press.

Loveless, Natalie. (2019). *How to Make Art at the End of the World: A Manifesto for Research Creation*. Durham, NC: Duke University Press.

Madison, D. Soyini. (2005). *Critical Ethnography: Methods, Ethics, and Performance*. New York: Sage.

Mahmood, Saba. (2011). *Politics of Piety: The Islamic Revival and the Feminist Subject*. Princeton, NJ: Princeton University Press.

Mancia, Lauren. (2019). *Emotional Monasticism: Affective Piety at the Eleventh-Century Monastery of John of Fécamp*. Leeds: Manchester University Press.

Mancia, Lauren. (2023). *Meditation and Prayer in the Eleventh- and Twelfth-Century Monastery: Struggling towards God*. Amsterdam: ARC Humanities Press.

Mariani, Angela. (2017). *Improvisation and* Inventio *in the Performance of Medieval Music*. New York: Oxford University Press.

Mason, David V. (2018). *The Performative Ground of Religion and Theatre*. New York: Routledge.

Massumi, Brian and Erin Manning. (2014). *Thought in the Act: Passages in the Ecology of Experience*. Minneapolis: University of Minnesota.

McCrary, Charles. (2022). *Sincerely Held: American Secularism and Its Believers*. Chicago, IL: University of Chicago Press.

McCutcheon, Russell. (2003). *Manufacturing Religion: The Discourse on Sui Generis Religion and the Politics of Nostalgia*. New York: Oxford University Press.

Melville, Gert and Markus Schürer, eds. (2002). *Das Eigene und das Ganze: Zum individuellen im mittelalter lichen Religiosentum*. Münster: Lit Verlag.

Meyer, Birgit. (2015). How to Capture the "Wow": R.R. Marett's Notion of Awe and the Study of Religion. *Journal of the Royal Anthropological Institute*, 22, pp. 7–26.

Miller, Patricia Cox. (2012). *The Corporeal Imagination: Signifying the Holy in Late Ancient Christianity*. Philadelphia: University of Pennsylvania Press.

Mitterauer, Michael. (2010). *Why Europe: The Medieval Origins of Its Special Path*. New York: Oxford University Press.

Morgan, David, ed. (2009). *Religion and Material Culture: The Matter of Belief*. New York: Routledge.

Moxey, Keith. (2013). *Visual Time: The Image in History*. Durham, NC: Duke University Press.

Nelson, Robert. (2007). Empathetic Vision: Looking at and with a Performative Byzantine Miniature. *Art History*, 30, pp. 489–502.

Newman, Barbara. (2005). What Did It Mean to Say I Saw? The Clash between Theory and Practice in Medieval Visionary Culture. *Speculum*, 80 (1), pp. 1–43.

Newman, Barbara. (2021).*The Permeable Self: Five Medieval Relationships*. Philadelphia: University of Pennsylvania.

Newman, Martha. (2020). *Cistercian Stories for Nuns and Monks: The Sacramental Imagination of Engelhard of Langheim*. Philadelphia: University of Pennsylvania.

Noble, Thomas F. X. (2009). *Images, Iconoclasm, and the Carolingians*. Philadelphia: University of Pennsylvania Press.

Noland, Carrie. (2009). *Agency and Embodiment: Performing Gestures/ Producing Culture*. Cambridge, MA: Harvard University Press.

Novick, Peter. (1988). *That Noble Dream: The "Objectivity Question" and the American Historical Profession*. New York: Cambridge University Press.

Nyong'O, Tavia. (2009). *The Amalgamation Waltz: Race, Performance, and the Ruses of Memory*. Minneapolis: University of Minnesota Press.

O'Doherty, Brian. (1976). *Inside the White Cube: The Ideology of the Gallery Space*. Berkeley: University of California Press.

Ono, Yoko. (2000). *Grapefruit: A Book of Instructions and Drawings*. New York: Simon and Schuster.

Overlie, Mary. (2016). *Standing in Space: The Six Viewpoints Theory and Practice*. New York: Six Viewpoints Institute.

Page, Sarah-Jane and Katy Pilcher, eds. (2021). *Embodying Religion, Gender, and Sexuality*. New York: Routledge.

Peers, Glenn. (2020). *Animism, Materiality, and Museums: How Do Byzantine Things Feel?* Leeds: ARC Humanities Press.

Peers, Glenn. (2024). *Byzantine Media Subjects*. Ithaca, NY: Cornell University Press.

Pelligrini, Ann. (2009). Feeling Secular. *Women and Performance: A Journal of Feminist Theory*, 19 (2), pp. 205–218.

Pentcheva, Bissera V. (2020). Performative Images and Cosmic Sound in the Exultet Liturgy of Southern Italy. *Speculum*, 95 (2), pp. 396–466.

Pickup, Martin. (2015). Real Presence in the Eucharist and Time Travel. *Religious Studies*, 51 (3), pp. 379–389.

Polanyi, Michael. (1974). *Personal Knowledge: Towards a Post-Critical Philosophy*. Chicago, IL: University of Chicago Press.

Pollack, Della. (1998). Performative Writing. In *The Ends of Performance*, Peggy Phelan and Jill Lane, eds. New York: New York University Press, pp. 73–104.

Pollack, Della, ed. (2005). *Remembering: Oral History Performance*. New York: Palgrave Macmillan.

Postlewait, Thomas. (2009). *The Cambridge Introduction to Theatre Historiography*. New York: Cambridge University Press.

Powell, Amy Knight. (2023). Zoe Leonard's Suitcases. In *L'art medieval est-il contemporain? Is Medieval Art Contemporary?* Charlotte Denoël, Larisa Dryansky, Isabelle Marchesin, and Erik Verhagen, eds. Turnhout: Brepols, 224–243.

Preston, Carrie J. (2016). *Learning to Kneel: Noh, Modernism, and Journeys in Teaching* (Modernist Latitudes). New York: Columbia University Press.

Promey, Sally. (2017). Foreword. In *Religion in Museums: Global and Multidisciplinary Perspectives*, Gretchen Buggeln, Crispin Paine, and S. Brent Plate, eds. New York: Bloomsbury, pp. xix–xxv.

Rider, Jeff. (2015). The Middle Ages Are within Your Grasp: Motor Neurons, Mirror Neurons, Simulacra, and Imagining the Past. *Studies in Medievalism*, XXIV, pp. 155–175.

Roach, Joseph. (1996). *Cities of the Dead: Circum-Atlantic Performance*. New York: Columbia University Press.

Rosenwein, Barbara. (2006). *Emotional Communities in the Early Middle Ages*. New York: Cornell University Press.

Rüpke, Jörg. (2016). *On Roman Religion: Lived Religion and the Individual in Ancient Rome*. Ithaca, NY: Cornell University Press.

Schaefer, Donovan O. (2015). *Religious Affects: Animality, Evolution, and Power*. Durham, NC: Duke University Press.

Schaefer, Donovan O. (2022). *Wild Experiment: Feeling Science and Secularism after Darwin*. Durham, NC: Duke University Press.

Schechner, Richard. (1985). *Between Theater and Anthropology*. Philadelphia: University of Pennsylvania Press.

Schechner, Richard. (2001). What Is "Performance Studies" Anyway? In *New Approaches to Theatre Studies and Performance Analysis*, Günter Berghaus, ed. Berlin: Max Niemeyer Verlag, pp. 1–11.

Schleif, Corine and Volker Schier. (2009). *Katerina's Windows: Donation and Devotion, Art and Music, as Heard and Seen in the Writings of a Birgittine Nun*. University Park, PA: Penn State University Press.

Schneider, Rebecca. (2011). *Performing Remains: Art and War in Times of Theatrical Reenactment*. New York: Routledge.

Schneider, Rebecca. (2014). *Theater & History*. New York: Springer.

Scott, Joan Wallach. (1991). The Evidence of Experience. *Critical Inquiry*, 17 (4), pp. 773–797.

Sergi, Matthew. (2020). *Practical Cues and Social Spectacle in the Chester Plays*. Chicago, IL: University of Chicago Press.

Seth, Vanita. (2024). (Un)Doing History: A Case for Epistemological Alterity. *History and Theory*, 63 (1), pp. 112–136.

Sharpe, Christina. (2016). *In the Wake*. Durham, NC: Duke University Press.

Shifrin, Susan. (2023). *The Museum as Experience: Learning, Connection, and Shared Space*. Leeds: ARC Humanities Press.

Smail, Daniel Lord. (2021). Foreword. In *Decolonizing "Prehistory": Deep Time and Indigenous Knowledges in North America*, Gesa Mackenthun and Christen Mucher, eds. p. 8.

Smith, Bonnie G. (1998). *The Gender of History: Men, Women, and Historical Practice*. New York: Cambridge University Press, pp. ix–xii.

Smith, Linda Tuhiwai. (1999). *Decolonizing Methodologies: Research and Indigenous Peoples*. London: Zed Books.

Smith, Pamela H. (2022). *From Lived Experience to the Written Word: Reconstructing Practical Knowledge in the Early Modern World*. Chicago, IL: University of Chicago Press.

Smith, Pamela H., Amy R. W. Meyers, and Harold J. Cook, eds. (2017). *Ways of Making and Knowing: The Material Culture of Empirical Knowledge*. Chicago, IL: University of Chicago Press.

Sonntag, Jörg. (2011). On the Way to Heaven: Rituals of *Caritas* in High Medieval Monasteries. In *Aspects of Charity: Concern for One's Neighbor in Medieval Vita Religiosa*, Gert Melville, ed. Berlin: Lit Verlag, pp. 29–55.

Sontag, Susan. (1966). *Against Interpretation*. New York: Farrar, Straus, Giroux.

Soussloff, Catherine M. (2000). Like a Performance: Performativity and the Historicized Body from Bellori to Mapplethorpe. In *Acting on the Past: Historical Performance across the Disciplines*, Mark Franco and Annette Richards, eds. Middletown, CT: Wesleyan University Press, pp. 69–98.

Spatz, Ben. (2015). *What a Body Can Do*. New York: Routledge.

Spatz, Ben. (2020). *Blue Sky Body: Thresholds for Embodied Research*. New York: Routledge.

Spiegel, Gabrielle M. (1997). *The Past as Text: The Theory and Practice of Medieval Historiography*. Baltimore, MD: Johns Hopkins University Press.

Sponsler, Claire. (2017). From Archive to Repertoire: The *Disguising at Hertford* and Performance Practices. In *Medieval Theatre Performance: Actors, Dancers, Automata, and Their Audiences*, Philip Butterworth and Katie Normington, eds. Suffolk: DS Brewer, pp. 15–34.

Sterk, Andrea and Nina Caputo, eds. (2014). *Faithful Narratives: Historians, Religion, and the Challenge of Objectivity*. New York: Cornell University Press.

Sternhell, Yael A. (2023). *War on Record: The Archive and the Afterlife of the Civil War*. New Haven, CT: Yale University Press.

Stoller, Paul. (1997). *Sensuous Scholarship*. Philadelphia: University of Pennsylvania Press.

Strukus, Wanda. (2011). Mining the Gap: Physically Integrated Performance and Kinesthetic Empathy. *Journal of Dramatic Theory and Criticism*, 25 (2), pp. 89–105.

Swift, Christopher. (2011). A Penitent Prepares: Affect, Contrition, and Tears. In *Crying in the Middle Ages: Tears of History*, Elina Gertsman, ed. New York: Routledge, pp. 79–101.

Symes, Carol. (2007). *A Common Stage: Theater and Public Life in Medieval Arras*. Ithaca, NY: Cornell University Press.

Symes, Carol. (2016). Liturgical Texts and Performance Practices. In *Understanding Medieval Liturgy*, Helen Gittos and Sarah Hamilton, eds. New York: Routledge, pp. 239–267.

Taves, Ann. (2000). *Fits, Trances and Visions: Experiencing Religion and Explaining Experience from Wesley to James*. Princeton, NJ: Princeton University Press.

Taylor, Charles. (2018). *The Ethics of Authenticity*. Cambridge, MA: Harvard University Press.

Taylor, Diana. (2003). *The Archive and the Repertoire: Performing Cultural Memory in the Americas*. Durham, NC: Duke University Press.

Trilling, Lionel. (1973). *Sincerity and Authenticity*. Cambridge, MA: Harvard University Press.

Troyano, Alina. (2000). *I, Carmelita Tropicana: Performing between Cultures* (Bluestreak). New York: Beacon Press.

Tullet, William, Inger Leemans, Hsuan Hsu, et al. (2022). AHR History Lab: Smell, History, and Heritage. *American Historical Review*, 127 (1), pp. 261–308.

Turner, Victor. (1982). *From Ritual to Theatre: The Human Seriousness of Play*. New York: PAJ, pp. 7–60.

Umbach, Maiken and Mathew Humphery. (2018). *Authenticity: The Cultural History of a Political Concept*. New York: Palgrave Macmillan.

Vitz, Evelyn. (2014). "The Seven Sleepers of Ephesus": Can We Reawaken Performance of This Hagiographical Folktale? In *Medieval and Early Modern Performance in the Eastern Mediterranean*, Arzu Öztürkmen, Evelyn Birge Vitz, eds. Turnhout: Brepols, pp. 89–121.

Weigert, Laura. (2015). *French Visual Culture and the Making of Medieval Theater*. New York: Cambridge University Press.

Wiles, David. (2003). *A Short History of Western Performance Space*. New York: Cambridge University Press.

Wood, Ian and G. A. Loud, eds. (1991). *Church and Chronicle in the Middle Ages*. London: Bloomsbury Academic.

Woolf, Daniel. (2019). *A Concise History of History: Global Historiography from Antiquity to the Present*. New York: Cambridge University Press.

Yardley, Anne Bagnall. (2006). *Performing Piety: Musical Culture in Medieval English Nunneries*. New York: Palgrave.

Acknowledgments

I am so grateful for the enthusiastic care that Piroska Nagy, Mark Smith, and especially Rob Boddice have provided as editors of this Histories of Emotions and the Senses series. Thanks are also due to the two anonymous reviewers of this manuscript, whose advice has only made this Element stronger, and to the whole team at Cambridge Elements, who speedily shepherded this Element through production.

This project started during a sabbatical from Brooklyn College in 2023–2024, and I am indebted to my colleagues in the History Department, and to my chairs, Philip Napoli and Steven Remy, who supported my leave and this project.

I spent that magical sabbatical year as a Visiting Scholar in the Performance Studies Department at New York University Tisch School of the Arts, which could not have happened without the hard work of André Lepecki and Alexandra Vasquez, or the initial encouragement of Adam Gidwitz, Raquel Otheguy, and especially Brandon Woolf. This Element formed over the course of that year, as I took classes with Misty De Berry, Karen Finley, Jeannine Tang, Alex Vasquez, and Allen Weiss; it was hashed out over conversations with Andrew Albin, María José Arjona, Emma Bartel, Courtney Bender, Deborah Black, Peggy Brown, Greg Bryda, Virginia Burrus, Caroline Bynum, Mike Chin, Eleonora Batista Fabião, Amir Farjoun, Kat Geng, Cam Grey, Fiona Griffiths, Brooke Holmes, Saleema Josey, Rosa Lambert, Patricia Lewy, Erika Lin, Namita Manohar, Sara McDougall, Elayne Oliphant, Donovan Schaefer, Matthew Sergi, Brian Sowers, Karen Stern, Jill Stevenson, Carol Symes, Kyle Thomas, Sophia Trainor, and Nancy Wu; it was given shape thanks to speaking invitations by Claire Bishop, Matthew Engelke & Justine Ellis, Nicola Masciandaro, Donovan Schaefer, and Sarah Gerth van den Berg; and it was made stronger thanks to audiences at the Rewald Seminar in Art History at the CUNY Graduate Center, the Institute for Religion and Public Life at Columbia, the Annual Medieval and Renaissance Forum at Keene State College, the Performance Studies Department at NYU, the Steven Northrop Dunning Memorial Lecture on Religious Thought at the University of Pennsylvania, and the LAMEM colloquium at Brooklyn College. Special thanks also to the monks of Holy Cross Monastery in Poughkeepsie, New York.

The performance-lectures at The Met Cloisters that are described at the end of this Element could not have happened without the support and the open-mindedness of Christina Westpheling, Aminah James, and The Met Cloisters' Education Department; nor could it have happened without the VX Department or the Security staff at the museum (especially Leila Osmani, who took special care to look out for us during the events). It also could not have happened without Nancy Wu, who hired me initially. As a lecturer at The Met Cloisters for the past 21 years, and a visitor of the museum for far longer, The Met Cloisters has played an essential role in my development as a medievalist. This Element is dedicated to the people who have labored and will continue to labor to make that museum relevant, smart, beautiful, unique, safe, accessible, educational, aesthetically engaging, emotionally poignant, spiritually resonant, and indescribably magical, worthy of the medieval legacy that it preserves.

Cambridge Elements ≡

Histories of Emotions and the Senses

Series Editors
Rob Boddice
Tampere University

Rob Boddice (PhD, FRHistS) is Senior Research Fellow at the Academy of Finland Centre of Excellence in the History of Experiences. He is the author/editor of thirteen books, including *Knowing Pain: A History of Sensation, Emotion and Experience* (Polity Press, 2023), *Humane Professions: The Defence of Experimental Medicine, 1876–1914* (Cambridge University Press, 2021) and *A History of Feelings* (Reaktion, 2019).

Piroska Nagy
Université du Québec à Montréal (UQAM)

Piroska Nagy is Professor of Medieval History at the Université du Québec à Montréal (UQAM) and initiated the first research program in French on the history of emotions. She is the author or editor of fourteen volumes, including *Le Don des larmes au Moyen Âge* (Albin Michel, 2000); *Medieval Sensibilities: A History of Emotions in the Middle Ages*, with Damien Boquet (Polity, 2018); and *Histoire des émotions collectives: Épistémologie, émergences*, expériences, with D. Boquet and L. Zanetti Domingues (Classiques Garnier, 2022).

Mark Smith
University of South Carolina

Mark Smith (PhD, FRHistS) is Carolina Distinguished Professor of History and Director of the Institute for Southern Studies at the University of South Carolina. He is author or editor of over a dozen books and his work has been translated into Chinese, Korean, Danish, German, and Spanish. He has lectured in Europe, throughout the United States, Australia, and China and his work has been featured in the New York Times, the London Times, the Washington Post, and the Wall Street Journal. He serves on the US Commission for Civil Rights.

About the Series

Born of the emotional and sensory "turns", Elements in Histories of Emotions and the Senses move one of the fastest-growing interdisciplinary fields forward. The series is aimed at scholars across the humanities, social sciences, and life sciences, embracing insights from a diverse range of disciplines, from neuroscience to art history and economics. Chronologically and regionally broad, encompassing global, transnational, and deep history, it concerns such topics as affect theory, intersensoriality, embodiment, human–animal relations, and distributed cognition. The founding editor of the series was Jan Plamper.

Cambridge Elements

Histories of Emotions and the Senses

Elements in the Series

Academic Emotions: Feeling the Institution
Katie Barclay

Sensory Perception, History and Geology: The Afterlife of Molyneux's Question in British, American and Australian Landscape Painting and Cultural Thought
Richard Read

Love in Contemporary Technoculture
Ania Malinowska

Memes, History and Emotional Life
Katie Barclay and Leanne Downing

Boredom
Elena Carrera

Marketing Violence: The Affective Economy of Violent Imageries in the Dutch Republic
Frans-Willem Korsten, Inger Leemans, Cornelis van der Haven and Karel Vanhaesebrouck

Beyond Compassion: Gender and Humanitarian Action
Dolores Martín-Moruno

Uncertainty and Emotion in the 1900 Sydney Plague
Philippa Nicole Barr

Sensorium: Contextualizing the Senses and Cognition in History and Across Cultures
David Howes

Zionism: Emotions, Language, and Experience
Ofer Idels

Affective Touching: Neurobiology and Technological Applications
Mark Paterson

Embodied Epistemology as Rigorous Historical Method
Lauren Mancia

A full series listing is available at: www.cambridge.org/EHES

For EU product safety concerns, contact us at Calle de José Abascal, 56–1°, 28003 Madrid, Spain or eugpsr@cambridge.org.

www.ingramcontent.com/pod-product-compliance
Ingram Content Group UK Ltd.
Pitfield, Milton Keynes, MK11 3LW, UK
UKHW021326180426
11947UKWH00017B/1455